UP THE BEN WI' EDDIE

by

Jimmy Jardine

To "Dad" (Donnie)
with best wishes
from Jimmy

Charles Kennedy, MP

I see Ben Nevis every day at home at Lochyside; it is a permanent fixture in my life! The view never fails to stir and impress me, and I can well understand how it motivates many to walk, climb and run up the Ben. My Grandfather Donald Kennedy, who was a Lovat Scout in the Great War, ran up the Ben regularly as part of his training regime. He was an "all rounder" - the equivalent of today's modern pentathlete - he competed all over the UK, and in 1916 he saw off all comers to win the Army championship in Perth. His brother Ewan, who farmed at Inverlochy, was also a notable athlete, and another of his brothers, my Great Uncle Willie, won the hammer throwing competition at the Cowal Games at the age of 64! Although their athletic genes do not seem to have passed to me an acute awareness of sporting prowess has always been in the blood!

Seriously, I knew Eddie well even though his Golden Era in the 1950s, when he shared the winning honours year in year out with another hill running legend Brian Kearney, was before I was born. For a while, before Eddie married Chrissie, we lived in Lochyside albeit at opposite ends. As families, we went to school together. He continued to train and run competitively until the mid nineties and he was a well kent figure, out training and road running, on the Blar and on Belford Road summer and winter. His achievement of completing 44 races, and winning three, on the UK's highest mountain which, in my opinion requires the pinnacle of grit and determination, and is the supreme challenge of fitness of any medium distance race in the country, is unsurpassed to this day. He is a legend in Lochaber, he has set the standard for, and inspired, new generations of hill runners (and Lochaber Athletic Club has produced a wealth of great athletes), and he deserves this book which is not only a tribute to Eddie but also records a wide range of material and events associated with the Ben.

Eddie died of cancer in 1996 and it is fitting that all the proceeds from Jimmy's book should go to Cancer Research. I am pleased to be associated with Jimmy's book and I commend it to you. It is a great read - about a good and gifted man.

Charles Kennedy MP
16 June 2005

Councillor Neil Cark,
Chairman, The Nevis Partnership

B EN NEVIS and Glen Nevis are cherished by the people of Lochaber and all who visit the area. The conservation, enhancement and management of the Nevis area are essential to safeguard its landscapes, wildlife and recreational opportunities, which bring enjoyment to the local community and employment to Fort William and Lochaber.

By supporting this book the Nevis Partnership is not only recognising the indominatable spirit of Eddie Campbell but is also demonstrating its support of all that is best within the wider Lochaber Community. *Up The Ben wi Eddie* is a grass roots, locally led project involving many local people all linking with their landscape, heritage and culture and valuing the importance of Ben Nevis, Glen Nevis and the surrounding area.

Of course, some of the activities recorded within the book are from a period when their environmental impacts were less well known and today might be too damaging to be considered. As a result *Up The Ben wi Eddie* also serves as an important historical record of the various events, stunts, dramas and adventures that have been the hallmark of people's involvement with Ben Nevis over many, many years.

Today there are approximately 450,000 visitors per annum into Glen Nevis and the need for the local communities to work together with landowners, conservation bodies and all the wider interest groups to manage the area's sustainability for the benefit of our future generations is of paramount importance. Perhaps we can all learn from Eddie Campbell's passion for Ben Nevis and work together in caring for its future.

Councillor Neil Cark,
Chairman, The Nevis Partnership

The members of the Nevis Partnership are:
The Highland Council, Scottish Natural Heritage, Fort William Community Council, sportscotland, Glen Nevis Residents Association, John Muir Trust, Lochaber Mountain Access Group, Inverlochy and Torlundy Community Council, Mountaineering Council of Scotland, Alcan Highland Estates, and Glen Nevis Estate. Forestry Commission Scotland and the Highlands of Scotland Tourist board are associate members.

Main cover photo courtesy of www.lochaber.com

INTRODUCTION

"*Come in, sit down and*

ceud mile failte

- a hundred thousand welcomes..."

ORAG AND KAREN of the Observatory Hotel's Gaelic greeting, pronounced "key-at meel-eh fall-cheh", promises you the very best of Highland hospitality wherever you go. On the right is a photograph of the actual seat at which earlier Ben Nevis ascenders could enter their thoughts in the Visitors' Book on reaching the summit. Now you will find nothing but ruins atop the mountain to welcome you – unless you bump into me looking for stories for *"Up The Ben wi' Eddie – 2"*! As the subtitle says, the idea of the book is photos and chat with people met on the ascent of The Ben following the Pony Track from the bottom to the top. Along the way there is some history and a bit more about the annual Ben Nevis Race than I'd intended! It is hoped the book will help give you a safe and enjoyable day out and, like me, you can share in the spirit and the smiles that "going up The Ben" brings – just look at the happy bunch at "Eddie's Bench"...

Above: *Eddie Campbell*
Right: *Clement Wragge*

It may seem strange to have *"Up The Ben wi' Eddie"* written by a Jimmy, but you will soon see why! Two names spring to mind whenever Ben Nevis is mentioned – Eddie Campbell (pictured left) and Clement Wragge (pictured right).

So why not *"Up The Ben wi' Clement"*? Well, for a start, you would need to rise at 0400 each day! Clement (or "Inclement" as he was nicknamed) set off to take daily weather readings at different points on the way up to the summit. As you will read later, this paved the way for the building of the Observatory and the Pony Track up to it. All this was over 120 years ago and you will be seeing the ruins of it at the top. Eddie would have been telling you himself if it hadn't been for the cancer, which caused his death in 1996 at the age of 64. He was always on The Ben, whether it be running up or standing handing out congratulatory certificates at the summit to those who made it up. "Made it up" may be the wrong choice of words when it comes to boasting about the time that one has taken to climb! You might hear of the track up to the summit being referred to as "The Tourist Route" – **No Way!** The Pony Track is a **Mountain Path** and the height, the distance, the weather and the terrain all have to be respected – see the next page's chart as to why! You have to be more prepared than the ones who enquire "Are we near the top?" just a few hundred yards from the car park! So please take time to read the Tourist Board's safety instructions overleaf. Most of the photos and people I talked to were in the summer months, but I started off in April '03, armed

with my digital camera. I'd got it from my workmates when I retired, although I did hesitate to use it in the beginning, as the instructions said not to get it wet! So there are a few favourite shots out-with the summer period and they show just how much of a change there is in conditions. **Going between October and May you <u>MUST</u> be fully equipped and fully competent** and you will see little crampon and ice axe warning signs to remind you at the respective out of season photos.

Good luck with your climb and I hope the weather is kind to you and you will get a clear day to see the stunning views from the top (only a hundred clear days in the year I'm afraid!). One of the most popular entries in the old Visitors' Book was "Missed the view, viewed the mist!" If you don't get a view, then this book will show you what it would have been like!

Jimmy Jardine, Avoch, 2005

WILL WE EVER LEARN ?

Then

A sunny day, with dry rocks and a balmy breeze can turn into an Arctic blizzard in seconds.

Until that gets through to everyone who ventures near the mountain, Nevis will go on claiming lives.

Now

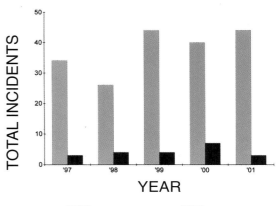

 Incidents 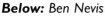 Fatalities

Below: Ben Nevis

3

Ben Nevis - BE SAFE !

For further information about climbing or walking up Ben Nevis, please visit www.lochaber.com website. There are many pages of information about Ben Nevis - including a live Ben Nevis WebCam. There is a forum for Ben Nevis at www.LochaberForum.com

Highlands of Scotland Tourist Board
Cameron Square
Fort William
PH33 6AJ
Tel: 01397 703781
Fax: 01397 705184

If you are thinking of attempting the ascent of Ben Nevis, please take the following factors into account:

The weather conditions can be atrocious at any time of the year and often bear no relation to the conditions down in the glens. During the winter the mountain is cloaked in snow and ice and in these conditions only mountaineers equipped with ice axes and crampons should attempt the ascent. Winter conditions can occur from October to May. During the summer months the weather can change with alarming speed and a sunny day out can quickly become a confused and disorientated struggle for survival. In anything other than stable and fine weather, you should not attempt the ascent unless: -

1. You have full waterproof clothing i.e. jacket and trousers.
2. You have warm clothing – top and bottom.
3. You have a warm hat and gloves or mitts.
4. You have substantial boots
5. You have a map (scale at least 1:50,000 and preferably 1:25,000).
6. You have a compass.
7. You know you have the ability to navigate accurately in mist and cloud under difficult conditions.

The round trip takes about 7 hours on average: 4 hours for the ascent and 3 hours for the descent. This timing does not allow for rests, food stops etc.

Always remember

People are killed on Ben Nevis every year. Those that die are not all mountaineers – some are ordinary summer walkers and visitors.

Do not put yourself in the position where you may be benighted.

Do not attempt the ascent alone – If a member of your group cannot continue, do not leave them to descend alone.

Do not allow yourself or any group member to become detached from your group.

DO NOT RELY ON MOBILE PHONES for your safety or security.

Yes we will learn !

ACKNOWLEDGEMENTS

THE BEN from Quinny's back garden in the evening after the Ben Nevis Race. I wish to thank all my friends, those of old and those who I have met through writing this book, for their help in making their collections and knowledge of The Ben available to me – sorry not naming them all individually. Special thanks to Alex Gillespie for all his photos, especially the double feature of "The Field of Cairns" – what an inspiration this is and looking at it will sustain you until you are up there in person! Thanks too, to John MacRae for his wit and wisdom and for living near the foot of The Ben with kettle and biscuits!

Photos, artwork and story copyrights remain with their owners. Any errors or omissions are my fault and I hope you can be in touch so I can set the record straight.

The old photos from when the Observatory was working are courtesy of the Royal Meteorological Society, which is the successor to the Scottish Meteorological Society. The Edinburgh Met Office was bequeathed many of the old snaps by Alexander Drysdale of Dollar, who acted as a relief Observer on many occasions. "The Granite House" in Fort William has a series of old postcards, which Alistair Ness has let me include. Nevisport gave me the use of the contour map and summit panorama chart and were very encouraging.

Fiona Marwick let me loose in the West Highland Museum! The newspapers over the years have a wealth of information and I thank them for use of cuttings I've accumulated.

A huge **"Thank you"** goes to authors of books on Ben Nevis for photos and stories: "Twenty Years on Ben Nevis" by Wm. T. Kilgour, 1905, which you could say was *"straight from the horse's mouth"* as he was there! "Ben Nevis – Britain's Highest Mountain" by Ken Crocket, 1986, a wonderful history of all aspects of The Ben for the Scottish Mountaineering Club. "The Ben Race – the supreme test of athletic fitness" by Hugh Dan MacLennan, 1994, for the Ben Nevis Race Association, who gave me use of all the information and pictures from the Ben Race programmes.

Nevisprint and my fund-raisers made the dream of "Up The Ben wi' Eddie" come true.

Below is Alistair MacMillan at the 25th Anniversary during the 70's of the Lochaber Athletic Club, of which he was President. He would shuttle us back and forward to the Aluminium Works' showers, dripping mud in his beautiful car after races before Claggan Park was built. Alistair died in 1994, but was so loved by all that his nickname will live on forever – even Prince Charles knew him by it – "Scoop". It is from him and his son Anthony in their days in "The West Highland News Agency" that most things come and I thank Anthony for their photographs. The 2 Ians - Ian "Roamer" Abernethy and Iain Ferguson have been a big help. It is so sad when deaths of personalities occur and there have been more since I started the book – hill people that you think are indestructible... Alver Burks, ex-RAF rescuer who let me use his photo album, George Smith, with a wealth of Ben Nevis experience and now Brian Kearney – in whose passing our main link with the past has been severed.

CONTENTS

Chapter 1

FREQUENTLY ASKED QUESTIONS

1. Which is Ben Nevis? 2. How do I get there? 3. How long will it take to climb?
And strangely, when I was asked to take a photo for a visitor halfway up the hill,
Does my bum look big in these trousers?

Which is Ben Nevis ?

THE EXTREMELY patient staff of the Nevis Bank Hotel dutifully come out many times a day to point out The Ben, just visible peeping over the shoulder of Melantee in the evening sunshine. It looks a long way away and it is! To get a good look at Ben Nevis you will have to go further afield from Fort William, because the lump of Cow Hill on the right of the photo and Melantee in front are in the way.

If you just wanted to see the Ben without any "hands on" climb, you could drive or take the bus up Glen Nevis, which is straight on at the roundabout from the Nevis Bank Hotel–you won't see the summit from there, but you will get a feel of its massive presence. Best views are from the Mallaig road and the Inverness road, both to the left at the Nevis Bank roundabout, especially if you like to see the dramatic cliffs of the north side. Without a car, footpaths will take you to adjoining villages of Inverlochy and Caol (pronounced cool) for stunning views.

An idea, if you don't want to walk, is to

board the ferry halfway along the bypass in Fort William and you will have an entire panorama of the The Ben towering above the rest. Eddie has a connection with this jetty – he would give advice to those who suffered from blisters from the climb, or more likely from the descent, to go and stand in the salty waters of Loch Linnhe on the ferry ramp. Taking the ferry is an ideal way for a photo shoot. Sail out either before or after making your climb with The Ben in the background. Then you can point out to your friends – been there, done that – definitely got the tee shirt!

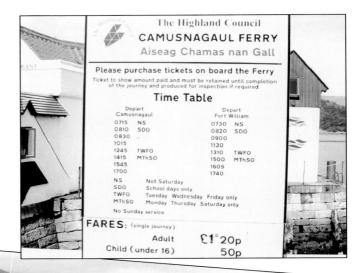

Viewpoint up Lundavra road (have 50p ready for telescope!).

APRES BEN

Deirdre, ready to rock!

8

See *how much the town has grown...*

1902

...*since this postcard*

It was sent to my grandfather by an American friend Lawson Ramage from Colorado. I looked up the Observatory Visitors' book for June 1902 to see if he'd put in any comment. They are now kept in the West Highland Museum, and I saw he'd written "Stiffer than Pike's Peak!". The postcard reads:

"6/24/02 Have been to summit - once is enough for me - It is 18 miles the round trip I was nearer heaven than ever before and perhaps as near as I will ever get - had the first clear day in 7 weeks - Lucky. Stop tomorrow in Inverness - wish you were here - Be good (and you will be lonesome) LR"

2003

How do I get there ?

OPTION 1 - THE VISITOR CENTRE

From the Nevis Bank Hotel you go straight ahead at the roundabout taking you into Glen Nevis. Situated about a mile and a half up the glen, the Visitor Centre is the ideal way to begin your climb up The Ben. This is the preferred option as there is good parking and a chance to look round the displays in the Centre giving you an idea of what is in front of you on the Ben Path. A chance to learn the **dos** and **don'ts** as you see from the poster! Importantly there are toilet facillities here, available from dawn to dusk all year. The Centre itself is open from the end of March to the beginning of November – dates and times on the notice boards. Signs will lead you downriver to the bridge, then cross over and go upriver and the path takes you round the outside of Achintee House and up onto the Pony Track where you will head uphill – without the ponies I'm afraid!

Photo courtesy of Royal Meterological Society

"Tom, Tom, Tom until I'm sick, sick, sick of them!"

Tom (Snr) giving me his wife's view of the naming of his ancestry from Campbeltown while Tom (Jnr) laughed. The pair had just crossed the bridge from the Visitor Centre and were heading off up-stream to The Ben. Tom (Snr) had had a quadruple heart bypass and was going to take it easy, although they had been walking in Nepal recently! Tom (Snr) told me he'd been ogling a beautiful Harley Davidson motorbike in the car park and pointed out the owner, disappearing along the track. I met the proud Japanese owner of the bike, and his friend Dave later on when they were admiring the "mighty" or rather "misty" chasm near the top. Dave was from Pembrokeshire and said he was finding it hard going as his only other mountain experience had been ascending Snowdon by train!

OPTION 2 - ACHINTEE

From the Nevis Bank Hotel turn left at the roundabout towards Inverness and then turn right just before the traffic lights into Claggan Road. Turn right just before Claggan Stores taking you onto the mile long single-track road to Achintee. Notice the cairn on the right – it explains about the Peace Cairn on the summit. You will pass the sports ground on the left where the Ben Nevis Race starts and finishes. If you are walking out from the town then go ahead at the roundabout into Glen Nevis and immediately turn left to go over the Old River Nevis Bridge, which will give you a wee short cut. This is the way the runners used to come before the Town Park was built in Claggan. Before 1971 the race started and finished at the King George V Park where the Leisure Centre now is. If you have an interest in the race then there is a magnificent display in the Leisure Centre about Eddie and the race. You can't take your car over this bridge as you see from the bollards and there has been many a "skint knee" for unwary runners not noticing them in the throng of about 200 as it was then. The race, 1st Saturday in September, is now limited to 500 runners.

Stop me and buy one!

Here is Rose, from New Zealand, on her way to work at Ben Nevis Inn ensuring customers get the very best wholesome food.

The ice cream sign (bottom right) is for the Ben Nevis Inn just off to the right of the car park at Achintee. It is your last chance for sustenance as from here-on-in the only snack you will get on The Ben is whatever you carry up with you – Photographer Alex Gillespie's Prime Rule of the mountains! My favourite quote of Alex's was in the very cold year of the Ben Race (1988) when Eddie and I arrived down at the halfway point together to where Alex was marshalling – 18 runners had been evacuated off by helicopter and Alex said *"Cold enough for you Eddie?"*

It is worth pausing at the information board before mounting the stile onto the Pony Track to study all the "gen" as the daily weather reports are extremely accurate. The Information Board also includes useful telephone numbers for your mobile phone, first on the list being the Fort William Police Station which is the link with the Lochaber Mountain Rescue Team should they ever be required – 01397 702361. Also heed the advice about thefts from cars and most certainly **do not do it!**

Looking back down, the Inn is a very welcome sight for weary Ben travellers on a hot day – a "thruppny" cone would go down very nicely thank you!

How do I get there ?
OPTION 3 - GLEN NEVIS YOUTH HOSTEL

To find the Youth Hostel you follow the same instructions as for the Visitor Centre but continue a mile further up the glen. As you can see there isn't much parking, but the main drawback for using this as a starting point for your ascent is the steepness of the path to join the Pony Track... **"Heart-attack Hill!"**

If you are resident here at the hostel or caravan site then it's your best bet. Where the path connects with the Pony Track it is quite a work of art in a spiral of stones.

Reaching the top of heartattack hill...

...are Mark and Christopher from Chesterfield who went up at some lick and continued at this pace all the way up the Pony Track! Ten years ago Mark was in a party climbing The Ben for Muscular Distrophy - they had two teams in a relay of six people at a time to each of the wheelchair users. It took fourteen hours and required a lot of one wheel work to negotiate many of the obstacles in the way – and there were many! The father & son bonding party are just joining the Pony Track at the top right end of the wood, while down at the Glen Nevis Caravan Park, a dad holds up one of the next generation of Ben climbers to see over the trees!

Don't come up this way to find The Ben...

...but did you ever ponder why there should be a Dudley Road in Fort William? Situated behind the Alexandra Hotel, the road commemorates the man who inaugurated the Peace Cairn at the summit of The Ben – Bert Bissell of Dudley.

Bert and his boys would go up annually and Bert himself had made over 100 ascents since 1945. He would give talks to the schools whilst up in Fort William. In his 90s he still went up, but sadly died in 1998. Bert has certainly earned his place of honour in the history of The Ben and can proudly sit on "Eddie's Bench" when the last tourist has left and the mountain is still.

How long will it take ?
Leaving the trickiest question till last, eh?

The answer of course is as long as a piece of string! In 1880 the man on the left, W.W. Naismith, the father of the Scottish Mountaineering Club, set off up The Ben 3 years before the Pony Track was built. His party, consisting of himself and 2 ministers, took 9 hours. They left at 9am on 1st May and returned at 6pm, but had no guide to take them through the mist and snow. They spent a couple of hours (including a near accident) "glissading" with their walking sticks hoping the mist would clear, but it didn't. So take away those 2 hours and you get the same answer of **4 hours up and 3 hours down**, which is exactly the expected time that one takes. Willie went on to publish his Naismith's Rule for working out the approximate time an expedition in the hills would take. Here is where the piece of string (or boot lace) comes in, because all we need to do is to measure up the path on the map and count up the height covered, then apply the formula:

One hour for every 3 miles with an additional hour for every 2,000ft of ascent.

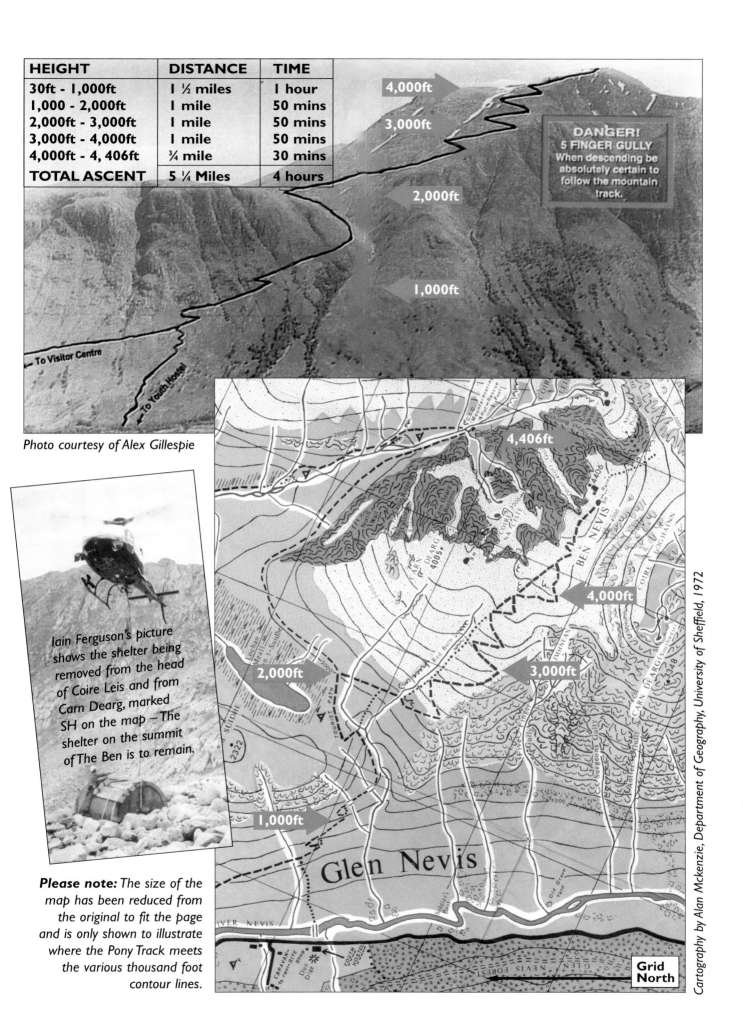

HEIGHT	DISTANCE	TIME
30ft - 1,000ft	1 ½ miles	1 hour
1,000 - 2,000ft	1 mile	50 mins
2,000ft - 3,000ft	1 mile	50 mins
3,000ft - 4,000ft	1 mile	50 mins
4,000ft - 4,406ft	¾ mile	30 mins
TOTAL ASCENT	5 ¼ Miles	4 hours

4,000ft

3,000ft

2,000ft

1,000ft

**DANGER!
5 FINGER GULLY**
When descending be absolutely certain to follow the mountain track.

To Visitor Centre

To Youth Hostel

Photo courtesy of Alex Gillespie

Iain Ferguson's picture shows the shelter being removed from the head of Coire Leis and from Carn Dearg, marked SH on the map – The shelter on the summit of The Ben is to remain.

Please note: The size of the map has been reduced from the original to fit the page and is only shown to illustrate where the Pony Track meets the various thousand foot contour lines.

4,406ft

4,000ft

3,000ft

2,000ft

1,000ft

Glen Nevis

Grid North

Cartography by Alan Mckenzie, Department of Geography, University of Sheffield, 1972

Chapter 2

LET'S GO
"UP THE BEN WI' EDDIE"
0 feet to 1,000ft

EDDIE IS pictured heading up The Ben from Achintee for yet another training run - can you imagine that he had to ask where Achintee was before his first Ben Nevis practice? Here are his own words of how it all began…

"I remember edging or sidling along the touchline at a shinty match being played at Keppoch, Roy Bridge, till I was standing next to Jock Petrie, who had been pointed out to me. I had been told that he was the man to see about running in the Ben Race and on asking if I could run in it, Jock, who was keenly watching the match, glanced down at me, asked me my name and grunted something like, 'If you want to run in the Ben Nevis Race, be at Achintee at half past five tomorrow morning (Sunday).' While taken aback at the abrupt answer, I was delighted, said thanks and then I had to ask where Achintee Farm was!"

Not quite zero – Eddie is about 250ft above sea level.

Even the Rocks get rusty!

I know Fort William has the reputation of being wet, but not that wet! Near the start of the Pony Track you will notice the water running down the path is a rusty brown colour. Old maps used to mark this as "Chalybeate" (containing iron). Now I am making no claims about the curative properties of this spring, but if you do go up on crutches, remember to bring them home – don't just leave them lying about on The Ben!

One thing that is certain, though, is that if you would like a deep refreshing sleep with pleasant relaxing dreams, you should gather a bit of Bog Myrtle from the side of the road as you make your way up to Achintee – it looks like this…

Rub the leaves and place them under your pillow – the scent is sublime. But don't chew them as they are toxic – you don't want to finish up on crutches! A few folk have wondered about the oily rainbow colours around stones in the same place on the path.

It's not ghostly drips of oil from the cars driven up years ago – it's only tinges of "peatrolium" seeping from the peat banks.

The car going up The Ben shown here in 1928 is a Baby Austin. The same man driving it, George F. Simpson from Longniddry, was back in Fort William 40 years later for the start of the 1968 Ben Nevis Race. He didn't go up The Ben this time! The car he was sitting in was a replica – George was still intact! In 1978, Esso presented George with a silver salver to commemorate the 50th annivesary of his Ben ascent. It was their forebearer that supplied the fuel for the car – Pratt's Perfection Spirit!

George, the Hon. Life President of the Scottish Austin 7 Club, died in 1991.

Stylish!

The Johnstons and the Petersons are Americans from Indiana and Glasgow, coming to see the path in the hope of going up one day. The brave little soldier in the middle took a tumble off the stile and landed face down on his glasses. Thankfully he was OK. It reminded me of a time Eddie had been training on The Ben and was crossing the stile here, when he heard a faint shout from high up on Melantee on the rocks behind the family. **Eddie to the rescue!** Eddie went to investigate and discovered a young lad had gone up on his own and become "cragfast" after hurting his leg.

I've always known this as the deer fence because the stile is so high – there have been a good few different ones over the years! This is it in 1968, my first Ben Race, where runners are just surging over the gate. Mike Davies, on the left of the photo with both hands on the gate, ready to spring over, won the race. He was a Reading schoolteacher and like so many others would come and train with Eddie on The Ben in the weeks before the race.

The gentle slope between the two stiles, Achintee and this one, acts as a nice gradual introduction to the hill after completing the mile long road from Claggan Park – especially if you've gone off too fast. One comment from a young spectator is etched in my mind for all time – *"Look at the state of that one – already!"*

Photo courtesy of Grace Paton who opened the 2004 Mountain Film Festival in Fort William in February. She and her late husband Andrew covered the Ben Race for an article in The Scots Magazine, Sept 1972, entitled "A Race for Supermen"!

And this, my brother, is The Ben

Two brothers from Galashiels are viewing the path for a possible climb the next day if the weather was to be better (it wasn't!). Neil in the red anorak has still to climb The Ben, but his brother has already been up and is putting Neil's mind at rest by describing it as "awesome!"

Over the stile is a good opportunity to identify the hills around you in Glen Nevis:-

The Ben itself (left of Carn Dearg SW) is 1,000ft higher than these surrounding hills.

Carn Dearg Southwest,
3348ft
Red stony summit

Melantee,
2322ft
Hill of the seat
←

Sgùrr a' Mhàim, 3601ft
(Scooravime)
Peak of the large round hill

Stob Bàn,
3274ft
White Peak

Mullach nan Coirean, 3077ft
Summit of the Little Corries →

"My wife doesn't understand me"

How often have we heard that line - but in this case it is true. Jane, my wife, had just been reading John MacRae's "A verse on The Ben" where it's mentioned that he had an epic Ben run when bent double. She said he could have done himself a permanent injury running like that – why did he not just retire? I leapt to John's defence and said that it would be nothing that wouldn't have healed up by the following September's Ben Race! Another thing that got her started is the photo on the right – in particular the man on the left...

These two lads are firemen from Newcastle, Jeff and his friend Graeme (be sure to spell it "ae" he says although the computer doesn't like it!) pictured near the foot of The Ben. Jeff had only just come off his mobile phone and announced proudly that he'd become a father! Doesn't the look sum it all up? I congratulated him and said he'd definitely spoken to the right person to publicise it! Telling Jane later, she was indignant. Here is a watered down version of what she said: "Typical man! Up The Bloomin' Ben while his wife does all the labour!" I told you she doesn't understand.

These Belgian scouts made a real splash of colour as they wound their way down the path after a trip into the clouds. Take heart though, because sometimes you will rise above the clouds into sunshine with the fabulous experience of a carpet of cotton wool with the highest peaks peeping through.

Photo courtesy of Noel Williams

Trainee Rescue Dog, Jodie...

...is having a look at The Ben. She comes from Crieff with her master Phil Gaskell. After a night-out in the '80s, Phil found he had rather rashly committed himself to doing the Ben Race and set out on a regime of fitness. He lasted fine almost the entire race, but suffered equipment failure when his leggings started falling down and he tripped up just before going onto the road at Achintee bursting his tendons. He said it was like running on a stump the mile down the road to the Town Park!

And who is the lady? Quite a family resemblance from 200 years ago – Elizabeth Gaskell the writer who worked with Charles Dickens.

A very well known runner suffered the same fate as Phil, but higher up The Ben near where Robert, Lee and "Barnaby" from Derbyshire are standing on their return from a misty top. They told me of the year in the Ben Race when Ron Hill, the famous marathon runner from Bolton had fallen on the descent from Halfway. Ron hurt his foot and had to hop the remainder of the way to the finish! Robert, left, had run against Ron Hill's son and knew the family well. Ron Hill Sports sold the innovative "string" vests designed by Ron to keep runners cool. Perhaps he got the idea from Eddie, who was famous for his "holy" vest. Walter Banks, the now retired long serving timekeeper for the Ben Nevis Race, caused great laughter when he presented Eddie with a new Lochaber vest – at the same time doubting if Eddie would ever wear it! Walter got the MBE for services to sport and the 2003 race was the first without him for many many years – it is not true that he has been made redundant by the trial of the new elecronic tagging system!

Another hot off the press masterpiece...

... from Marita from Holland who was painting the scene up towards "Eddie's Bench". We talked about hills and she said "Also The Three Sisters in Glencoe are very beautiful – it is not always the highest that is the best!"

"Very true" came a voice from behind and we were joined by Ranger Ian Donaldson on his way to work on the channels crossing the path higher up. Just the very man to take her under his wing as she was doubting herself in the low cloud ahead.

Marie and Barrat (left) from Kent, who I met just further on, had climbed The Ben 15 years ago when, unlike today, they'd had a wonderful view from the top. They'd come then to see the heather and the Highland Games with Sir Jimmy Savile, pictured below, marching in front of the Lochaber school pipe band on his way to open the 2004 Lochaber Games. So nothing has changed! "Except," said Barrat "we are 15 years older and have a son – Anthony."

Eddie's Bench has a customer...

It was at the First Melantee Zigzag that I came across the first member of this trio from Lincolnshire. I was coming past the junction with Heartattack Hill getting my camera out from all its protective layers of cases, in the hope that someone would be sitting on "Eddie's Bench" for a photo. Sure enough – there sat Shane. He told me that for the last 3 Bank Holidays he and his friends had done Snowdon, Scafell and now Ben Nevis. It wasn't going well for him and he was just enjoying relaxing while the others went on. I came across them higher up, Ray and Elliot, and they said the 500 mile journey was well worth it as they'd come through some beautiful countryside being used to total flatness at home.

Just to mention that you may notice when runners practise on The Ben, they will veer off the track at these rocks on the left in the photo below. It saves going round the zigzag at Eddie's Bench but you pay for it in steepness, wetness and slipperiness – at one point you are down in the depth of a head-high peat trough! A lot of the fun of The Ben is talking about the merits of the various shortcuts. At the prize-giving tea after the 1968 Halfway Ben Race, which was my introduction to hill running, all the visiting runners gathered round Eddie asking what route he recommended. "Just you ones keep behind me and I'll show you!"

"I'm Jonathan Darrock or Darro**ch** as you'd say up here!"

So said Jonathan, from Newport, South Wales, as he was having a refreshment on the way down at Eddie's Bench. He hadn't had a view from the top but had enjoyed the climb.

From the clouds...

...that robbed Jonathan of his view came these three Swiss lads. They'd also had a refreshment – but theirs had been Baileys! - A toast on the summit after singing the Swiss National Anthem. Their names are Ulsean, Floren and Martin.

Chapter 3

ONLY ANOTHER 3406FT — TO THE SUMMIT

1,000ft to 2,000ft

Don't look - they're taking a short cut!

Photo courtesy of Duncan McEwen.

Peter Colman (who's in there somewhere) has this to say in memory of Eddie... *"We at Vauxhall hold many fond memories of Eddie and one story that immediately springs to mind is the 1980 Ben Nevis Race. I remember looking for him just before the start, as I suppose many other competitors would do, and was next to him on the start line waiting for the gun. After an endless few minutes came the announcement that the race was cancelled due to weather conditions on the summit. Amid shock and disappointment the runners dispersed and Eddie invited me and some other Vauxhall runners to join him for a jog. 'Where are you going?' we asked. 'Up the Ben?'*

'Aye, to the top,' he replied, casually.

With 500 miles of driving the day before and only a haggis and a bottle of rare malt to show for it, I was soon trailing alongside him. Needless to say, in true Eddie style, we reached the summit and returned safely."

Eddie had often assisted the Vauxhall team to create records for the Three Peaks and in 1977 was seen to use a compass! Leen Volwerk's comment was – "It's a bluff!"

Look out for *Chrystals* on the path...

Colette and Chris Chrystal are on their way up The Ben for Eddie's 100 years of Ben running "race", negotiating the 2nd Melantee Zigzag. They are being very good and are not taking the badly eroded shortcut! Crystals and precious metals were to the fore on The Ben when a fantastic story broke in the Sunday Mail on 1st April 1979. It was discovered that the inner core of Ben Nevis was made up of an extremely rare and valuable ore called "Lirpaloof". This thistle-shaped revolving restaurant in the design on the left would be built on the top. Before that though, 300ft would have to be removed from the height of The Ben to keep it below the mist level so diners could take in the marvellous view. The snag with that is that now Ben Macdhui in the Cairngorms would be the highest mountain in Britain at 4248ft. Mountain man, Hamish MacInnes, was at first against it because of what it would do to The Ben. On reflection he admitted that there were many long-term employment opportunities. So did Sir Russell Johnston who was then the MP for Inverness-shire and a European Parliamentarian. He called it "visionary". That was the era of "Scotland's Oil!" and would it now be "Scotland's Ore!"? The material itself was so explosive that it could only be mined using rubber shovels! Rubber sided trucks would whiz down to Loch Linnhe carrying the ore, but the speed would be controlled by these special loops as shown in the diagram on the right. A better understanding of what was going on can be gathered from looking at the track in a mirror and noting the date of the paper!

(The wonderful April fool was by Tom Noble and Nick Hunter, with Hamish and Sir Russell's co-operation. Roy Petrie was the man behind the most admirable artwork)

Kieran from North Devon...

...was viewing the view up Glen Nevis at the second Melantee Zigzag. It was on the flat bit of ground in the distance that "Braveheart" was filmed. Kieran was on his way down after having climbed The Ben and thought it was magical, absolutely a wonderful place. He was doing a walking holiday and planned to go on to walks around Inverness. The washed-away bit at Kieran's right hand is known as the second short cut to the runners, but is slippery when wet - which is always. Here is Lochaber runner Dawn Scott training on The Ben. Dawn was the 2003 winner of the International Hill Race at Snowdon for Scotland in the women's event, and is just emerging at the other end of the short cut. We, however, shall stick to the path, for Zigzags are gentler!

Not long after this on the way up you will come to the three bridges. The last one is still known as "Broken Bridge" although it now boasts a beautifully safe aluminium one. It required a lot of dynamite between the "before" and "after" photos to make the levels of the path equal – there had been 6 feet difference in height and you had to scrabble up the rock on the far side going up. There was a big iron ring in the rock which you could swing on to get up if you took a big enough run at it over the bridge! The "before" picture is some of us Rover Scouts from Penicuik returning down after camping on the top in 1968. Dod here, nearest the camera and not one to be emotionally moved, had stood in awe the previous evening on the summit at the sun setting over the Cuillins: "You know," he said, "the sun waits for no one!"

One person who doesn't like the new bridges is Brian Finlayson seeing his lead in the race vanish when he got a stud caught in them, falling flat on his face!

Before

After

26

Single file

Devonians Sue and Dick had a long history of climbing. Dick was of the strong opinion that you should stick to the rule of his alpine days – never set off after lunchtime. He had noticed two lads who were still on their way up at the Halfway Loch, just sitting in the sun. He nearly exploded when hearing they'd asked me if there was a bar at the top!

Crocodile

Leen Volwerk leads his charge down The Ben. Leen is head of English at Lochaber High School and is an "ultra" distance runner along with his wife Pam. Each year they assist in the Ben Nevis Race. Pam is pictured here at the party after Eddie's Ben Nevis Centenary run in August 1994.

"Where are you and why is the kettle not on?"

"I'm directly opposite you now – underneath the helicopter!" I replied, trying to sound fairly normal.

The story starts when I met Lorna at the wooden bridge on the way up. She'd walked out from Fort William via the Visitor Centre and felt the route seemed a bit circuitous in the initial stages. On holiday from Edinburgh, she was doing The Ben then going on to Skye the next day. It didn't look too promising for a view from the top for seeing the famous Cuillin hills of the Misty Isle.

From about the Second Zigzag you disappeared into the clouds and it became wet, cold and windy. It was just above there that I encountered Lorna again as I was coming down. She was determined to get up, but a bit worried about finding her way in the mist, so I turned about to chum her. It's the first time I've escorted someone up and perhaps overdid the pointing out of all the features with their history and names I know them by as we passed them – "The Scuplted Well", "Adam's Rib" where the runners come up a ribbed shape track onto the tourist path at the end of the Third Zigzag; "Lover's Lane" shortcutting the Fourth Zigzag (so named because of a pair of underpants found at the scene) before "Black Rock"; then comes "The Field of Cairns" going straight up from "The Fank" which is a round shelter of rocks. The Field of Cairns is split in two by "The Almost Eternal Snows", which had all melted, then you pech up the steep "McLean's Steep" – a tight zigzagging of the track named after the road maker, bringing you to the "Outer Marker", as you see below, a pink ever-so-welcome-in-bad-weather splodge on a pole set in a cairn, and thence onto the summit, skirting the two gullies. Lorna admitted later that my lying about the distances from place to place had kept her going! I still had a full flask of tea as I hadn't tarried on the top earlier, so we shared that in the refuge shelter with clothes steaming when we got out of the rain. Lorna gave up rolling a fag with stiff fingers and reached in for one that was prepared earlier! Off we set down - past the Outer Marker, down McLean's Steep and onto the Upper Field of Cairns, etc, etc! Mist was billowing up in the Red Burn Gully as we arrived at the Halfway to have the rest of the flask. The waterfall prompted a call of nature, so Lorna disappeared back round the corner. I paced about, whistled tunelessly, studied rock formations, wrung out hat and gloves and at last she appeared again. Sodden jeans are very hard to get down - I'm told!

Underway again, we met five lads who were camping at the Halfway Loch and were heading back up to the Red Burn Crossing to fill their water containers with the "sweet" water that they had enjoyed when they'd drank there on their climb of the Ben earlier in the day. They

The Good

The Bad

were from all over – Claudio from Rome, Matt from Southampton, a Londoner and a Spaniard. They all laughed at their friend who introduced himself the wrong way round as Kent from Alex! It's the cold. They described their climb as "refreshing!"

Onward and downward past the lochan, down the Stairway to Heaven, round Windy Corner and back to the wooden bridge where I'd first met Lorna. In the gathering dark a figure approached, vigorously marching up towards us. Among his first words were to describe the spot where he found us: "This is *Car's Corner* where the famous photo was taken of the Ford that was driven to the summit in 1911!"

Re-reading this, one might feel that the whole day had been a bit too much information for poor Lorna! But in her turn, when she brings friends up, she can point into the mist and say authoritatively *"This is The Field of Cairns!"*

The Knight in Shining Armour was none other than John MacRae who'd seen my car still sitting in Fort William and wondered what was up. So up he had come with spare clothes and a flask – a real kind thought. Off we set again and soon we were looking down on the Glen Nevis caravan park, seeing a tiny light in the distance in the window of the caravan where I was staying that night. I phoned to say I'd be about another hour

and that's when I received my mild rebuke mentioned at the start as I was supposed to have had the tea prepared for the MacLeans, my hosts, arriving at 7.00 and it was now 9.00 pm. This is when the helicopter appeared on the scene! It was only on exercise but we beetled down before causing anyone any further worry. Here is a photo of John and Lorna as we neared his van at Achintee, so we soon had Lorna back at her B&B. She had plenty to write up for that day – *"Dear diary, are there no normal people on The Ben?"*

The photos of the car driven by Henry Alexander on the top of Ben Nevis were used for advertising in the early days of motoring to "further popularise the pastime of automobilism" as the Oban Times reported at the time. It certainly worked!

Nevisport have kept the tradition going with their ad saying *"Get into top gear"* but at least they have the decency to add "Scuse the horrible pun!"

Going up The Ben one day was a lad with cardboard hitch-hiker plates sticking out of his rucksac!

The Blairs were on The Ben!

Not Tony and Cheri, but John and Margaret. They were on their way back down the "Stairway to Heaven". The Blairs are from the Isle of Wight. John's tee shirt is of speedway and Margaret's the North York Moors where they often enjoy walking, but said they'd never attempted anything like this before!

This section in the photo below right is up from "The Windy Corner", where you leave the Glen Nevis side of Melantee and head up the Red Burn Gully. It is a well-made series of steps to prevent the path being worn away, demanding great concentration on the way down as you can see by the runners' faces. Roger Boswell, the Welsh Wizard, is leading as they leap and bound down. What does one do if you encounter a runner in such a place as this? There are warning signs when it's a race day, but generally you will hear the scrabbling of an approaching body well enough away to weigh up who's going where. On one occasion on my way down, I heard great thumpings behind me and stepped off the track to let whoever it was go past... I looked round just in time to see a huge rock hurtle by – well, a fairly big one which gets bigger by the telling!

John Coon flexes his muscles for "HIGH SPEED". John's wife Suse is author of "Race you to the Top".

Photo courtesy of Suse Coon.

Photo courtesy of "Up and Down" magazine.

I WONDER WHETHER ST COLUMBA...

..had a day like this, if he went up The Ben, on arriving at the head of Loch Linnhe after his voyage from Ireland in 563AD? Perhaps he struck it lucky and had a lovely view of the Antrim Hills from whence he'd come. He later went on up the Great Glen in a boat and saw Nessie, calming her with a blessing when she reared up. Eddie had that power too, as Leen Volwerk says in his introduction to his booklet "Eddie Campbell – An Appreciation"...   *"Often when I was out running along the road by the Caledonian Canal on summer afternoons I would see Eddie's mini-bus coming towards me. As he passed by he would always raise his right hand in greeting with a gesture which, combined with his white hair and patriarchal beard, always looked rather like a blessing. On reflection, it was. Mankind is diminished by his passing."*

I'm bursting to tell of my (Jimmy that is) experience of someone waving to me while I was jogging on Arthur's Seat in Edinburgh – Pope John Paul!

The family circle above, in grim weather near the summit of The Ben, is from Holland. They followed in St Columba's wake, sailing their yacht from Ireland to Fort William, after collecting their daughter Lynn in Dublin. They are musicians and here are the girls earlier on in the climb when just about to disappear into the cloud in the Red Burn Gully. The Captain has gone on ahead to spy out the land – making sure there is some! The ladies are Lynn, Ritta (mum) and Silviana.

Grandstand View...

...for the Portsmouth pair looking across the Red Burn Gully to where they were going to be in a couple of hours' time – out of the green and into the grey! They were getting a nice day with a good view. This is how the old Observatory guidebook described going up the Red Burn Gully... *"The road now turns to the left, and enters the short side valley of Coire na h-Urchairean. This is often the most trying part of the ascent; the valley is usually close and airless, and the stranger ascending for the first time finds it almost as difficult to reach the top of the corrie as to pronounce its name!"* Not everyone is lucky enough to have lived next door to Gaelic teacher Alisdair Grant: *"Corry nah hooruchurun"*(of the shots).

Carla had just put her jacket on when I next encountered them reaching the end of the third zigzag and about to burst forth onto the upper slopes where the wind was a little chilly. The loch in the hills to the left of the long inlet of Loch Linnhe is "Lochan Lùnn dà-Bhrà" (Lundavra). Householders over there still have a tradition of seeing-in the New Year 11 days after ours, never having changed from the "Julian" calendar!

Dear Editor...

In the above photo, Rangers Ian Donaldson (right) and his mate Francis McDade constantly battle against the Ben Path being washed away climatically and with the volume of 100,000 pairs of boots each year, particularly at this point (below) before going up to the Halfway Loch. Runners tend to plough onwards here at the head of the Red Burn Gully, contouring through the Green Burn and peat which is very unstable with a sky high erosion factor, plus the danger of getting lost when the mist's down. Best advice is... follow the arrow, not the *"Bloomin' Ben Runners"*!

The cheery person sitting at the "basket of stones", as the spot is known, is Paul from Newton Abbott in Devon. He was marshalling for the Vauxhall Four Peaks Challenge and they had the most ever teams – 58, so he was expecting to have 174

Letter courtesy of Ken Johnson at The Oban Times

competitors come his way in about half an hour's time. The Ben was the first of their peaks, then it was off to do Helvellyn, substitute for Scafell Pike because of poor parking space (required for 58 new Vauxhalls, one per team of three + driver!) and erosion on England's highest mountain. Next would come Snowdon before taking to the ferry for the Emerald Isle to finish on Corrán Tuathail (Crawn2hill) near Killarney on the Saturday – this was Thursday afternoon. The event run by the "Wooden Spoon" charity (British Rugby Union) will raise £300,000 for disabled and disadvantaged children. They shared The Ben that day with the "Three Peaks Yacht Race" which did include Scafell, parking not a problem as they cycled up from the yachts to the foot of the mountain. The "Wooden Spoon" name comes from the gift of such a utensil being given to English rugby fans after a drubbing in 1983's Five Nations tournament. The spoon was used to raise money to help youngsters fight mental and physical ailments with the positive statement of –

"We have met all these foes with good humour and much enjoyment!"

The Ranger Service asks that organisers of charity events follow the code of conduct and let them know of the plans for the event and to check on the availability of facilities. Then Rangers Ian and Francis can mark safe routes with flags because participants are tied to a certain day and can't pick and choose their weather. For the Ben Nevis Race in days gone by, yellow ochre used to be spread round the foot of cairns showing the direction for runners in the mist.

"Familiar squat cairns would loom up like friends,

Their yellow dye markings would show me the bends."

I was amused to see squiggly yellow marks in the snow round cairns early in the year, but didn't follow them!

New Vauxhall Ventoras in Fort William back in the 70's as Provost George Henderson congratulates the Vauxhall team on completion of "The Three Peaks" assisted by Eddie on The Ben and Joss Naylor on Scafell Pike. Eddie loved these 3 Peaks records and beat the Vauxhall time of 13hrs 43mins by 21mins with Ben Race Chairman George MacPherson driving in an E-type Jag. Joss had a time of 11hrs 52mins when he set the individual record – no wonder he is known as "The Incredible Joss"!

On race day Ian, member of the Lochaber Mountain Rescue Team, will position himself at the edge of the gully near the summit to prevent anyone taking their last shortcut – a vertical 2000ft straight down one!

I just had to ask these lads what the paddles were for and they told me they were from London University taking samples from the Halfway Loch and then going on to other West Highland lochs. We talked about midges and they said they got themselves completely enclosed in special suits like spacemen. It would be quite frightening to see them loom out of the mist towards you – *"Take-me-to-your-leader!"*

I reckon that the real reason for the paddles is what the coach couriers tell their

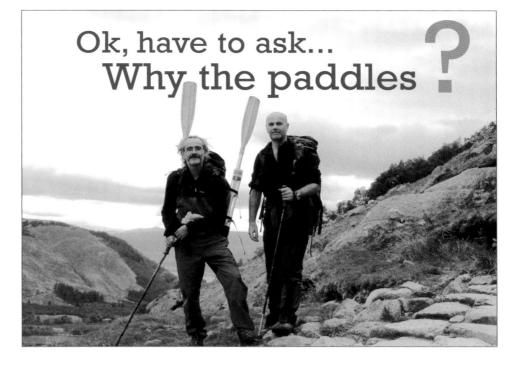

Ok, have to ask...
Why the paddles ?

passengers when they point out the gigantic pipes overhanging the town - for clearing lumps at the porridge factory inside the hill supplying the hotels by direct feed! Porridge is a very good deterrent (taken internally!) for the dreaded midges, as, through time, you get a build up of vitamin E next to your skin and they don't like it. Or you can use Avon's SSS (applied externally!) which has something in it that they can't stand and also has the added bonus of making you more acceptable to your fellow climbers! One day Fort William residents woke up to a huge curtain of water hanging in the sky and it was a kind of air lock in the tunnel in the bowels of Melantee. The tunnel is 15 miles long through the hills to Loch Treig and was built to bring water to the powerhouse of the Aluminium Factory. It was opened in 1930, being the largest tunnel in the world at that time. Fort William worthy, Alex Mackin, told me such progress didn't come without a price and he had lost an uncle and nearly his father in the construction. His father had just straightened up when a giant iron pinch bar crashed down from above and imbedded itself in the rock like "Excalibur" exactly where his head had been seconds earlier!

John (mine host) Macdonald about to take on the midges at grass-cutting

Photo courtesy of Alcan Primary Metal - Europe

Clitheroe Kids
Martin and Gordon...

...reminded me that Jimmy Clitheroe had died about 30 years ago! They summed up their climb by saying "they can't take it away from you!" The pair had been impressed by the effort it must have taken to carry all the stuff up to build the Observatory and wondered how anyone could have lived up there. One disappointment for them was not getting to see the dizzy drops over the edge at the top because of the cloud. When I encountered Leizle from Bloemfontein (pictured below earlier with Johan from Kimberley, South Africa) she was sitting alone on the edge of Tower Gully saying she was refusing to move until the mists cleared and she could see down! It is a fine spot and you are welcomed onto the summit by the snow bunting perched on a rock singing its little heart out...

"*I'll* do the flying round here if you *don't* mind!"

Photo courtesy of
Noel Williams

Photo courtesy of
Royal Meteorological Society

Who says Sir Cliff has no fans?

What do you reckon the above tablet means?

This flag bravely fluttering by the Halfway Loch was put there by Crossroads Carers of Lambeth, London.

Helping me to read the flag is Jonathan and here he is again in the photo below with his brother, Blair and their father, Paul, taking a breather on the final stretch up to the top. They were camping in Glen Nevis and the boys were looking forward to getting back down again to go jumping into the rock pools. Daddy said he was feeling a bit like one of the old pack horses with all the gear!

Chapter 4

THE HALFWAY WALL (JOHN'S WALL)
2,000ft to 3,000ft

Nice spot to stand and admire the view out over the Great Glen

Built by John Mathieson of the rescue team

EDDIE PERHAPS never came much to this wall, because runners always cut off the corner. He happily shared his intimate knowledge of The Ben shortcuts with others, among them being Dave Cannon, who says this of Eddie...

"I first met Eddie in July 1970 when I came to run the Half Nevis Race. It was by far the toughest race I had competed in and on the Sunday Eddie and his friends took us up for a training run to the top of The Ben. I said that there was no way that I would be back for the full Ben Race in September but due mainly to Eddie telling me I could do well in it, I did. I then came back every year until 1976 and achieved five wins, one second and one third. Over the years, my family and myself became very good friends with Eddie, Chrissie and their family. Even after I left fell-running to concentrate on the marathon and road running Eddie always gave me lots of encouragement to do well so I will always remember Eddie as a very good friend and as a man who helped me in my running career."

Dave still looks in on Chrissie and the family when he comes north from The Lakes. Just how well Eddie knew the Ben is still coming to light for me. I learned recently that in mist going up the Red Burn screes, he would keep going forward until he could no longer hear the water running underneath the stones, then he'd take a sharp right turn and come out smack on the Pony Track many places in front!

½ way

(Up The Ben that is - not through the book, you've still a long way to go for that!)

The Red Burn Crossing is halfway in height and distance – a good place to have a breather and reflect on what's past and what's still to come in the second half. Here's Bert Bissell gamely going on with his stick as Mary Gillespie administers a well known energy drink! Duncan Haggart on the left is accompanying the famous figure on one of Bert's annual visits to the summit with members of his Dudley bible study group.

11 year old Rhea (below) is proudly showing off her newly earned tee shirt with "Been there, done that" as they descend from the top. Alex points with grandfatherly pride as Neil and Scotty look on.

Inset photo is Alex' grand-daughter Caitlin having also conquered The Ben

Photos courtesy of Alex Gillespie

39

So *loud* was the *tinkling* of the *burn...*

...that we'd to shout to hear over it and I laughed when the lady said she was Hillary from South Wales but her husband Andy was English! She was thrilled with The Ben on her first visit and it had been an ambition of hers to climb it after having done Snowdon last year. Andy was on his first visit where he wasn't getting paid for it – "Aha," said I "Marines!"

Months later I said the same thing as I came down The Ben on a crisp day at the end of October. I'd seen tents pitched at the Halfway Loch and came across some very fit looking guys heading back towards them. "Marines" I'd thought again and then noticed one had blond hair tied up! It was Captain Philippa Tattersall, who had the whole nation rooting for her in her bid to become the UK's first ever female commando. She was in the news again just after her Ben expedition announcing she was writing a book about the toughness of her path to success, so we will all be able to share in what must have been a truly fantastic feeling when beating that "Tarzan" course with its 30 foot wall!

Captain Pip passes on some words of encouragement to draw on when you are on The Ben...

"You could be the fittest person in NATO, the sights, the sounds and atmosphere of The Ben will leave you breathless. One step at a time, you know your limits and capabilities and only you can have the inner drive and determination to achieve your goal."

And with that she was off for a well earned bath clutching her towel and radox – oh and razor saying, "Couldn't face the press with hairy legs!"

Gonna fly the flag!

Cort from North Carolina is pictured here with the Halfway Loch in the background. He is on the "zig" part of the First Zigzag making his way to the top to unfurl the Stars and Stripes. Doesn't look like there are any bathers in today but, on a really hot day, the lochan is a very tempting sight. In the winter time enthusiastic curlers would come up from Fort William to enjoy their sport – You can imagine the cries of ***"SOOP SOOP"*** ringing out in the valley between The Ben and Melantee as the sweepers vigorously "sooped" the path with their brooms for the roaring stone.

Anything to keep warm – unlike this spectator on the left! If Cort looks to his right from where he is standing, he will see the "mark of Zorro" as the Tourist Path bends back on itself after coming up the Red Burn Gully to go up to the Halfway Loch. In the early 1900s some scoundrels would ford the burn and come scrabbling up the steep hillside to the point where Cort is, just to avoid paying the shilling toll at the Halfway Hut! Jamie from London and Jonka from the Philippines in this photo (left) might have been employed as traffic wardens to collect these errant fees had they been born 100 years ago.

If you are doubting whether Jamie would make as good an enforcer as the famous Zorro, just see over the page! There is no trace anymore of the Halfway Hut, the auxiliary meteorological station. Here is a photo of the hut as it used to be, with an Observer about to awaken himself with the lovely cool water! It's an unusual picture for the old days as we are not used to seeing anyone on Ben Nevis in the 1800s without them being all happed up, complete with bowler hat and moustache!

"I have come here for peace!"

KenJutsu is a form of martial arts where the followers believe in the spiritual side of the sword as well as the movements. Jamie has been doing KenJutsu since aged six, following in his father's footsteps.

Jamie and Jonka had been enquiring how long it would take get up to the top and, since it was already 5 p.m., were a bit put off by the news that they'd only done one hour out of the seven it would take to get there and back. I pointed to the doublebass case on the banking beside them, "Musicians?"

Wrong! Jamie unzipped the case and took out his long Samurai's sword in its scabbard, then climbed rather perilously up the peaty hillside to go through his routine – breathtaking! He carefully tied the sword back in the scabbard before slip-sliding back down to the path. I thanked him for the demonstration and handed over a Mars bar – he'd have no problem splitting it in two!

Remember the famous lines from the TV show Kung Fu with David Carradine...

Listened for - they cannot be heard. **Looked for** - they cannot be seen.
Felt for - they cannot be touched, Grasshopper.

Also going up on a spiritual odyssey...

...(but without the swords!) was this trio on the right, heading up to the Halfway Wall. Tom from Stuttgart, Ron from The Philippines and Heekyeom from South Korea were religious students on a few days out from a London summer camp. They spoke of the moving experience it was going to be for them and they couldn't wait to stand on the highest point in the land. Zeal is a fine thing for putting a spring in your step but beware of the **"Ben Nevis Look"** where some poor souls have gone beyond the norm. Ben runner and Lake District champion Joss Naylor (left)

shows the determination in Tommy Orr's photo that allowed him to run up 60 peaks at 60 years of age in 1996 – 110 miles and 34,000ft of ascent in 35 hours raising over £16,000 for Multiple Sclerosis!

The mists were clearing..

..for Otto and Anna as they were coming down from their visit to "the highest point in the land". The Swedish pair had stopped to take a photo of the sun lighting up Carn Dearg behind them. They were on their honeymoon and I at once said *"Britain's highest kiss!"*

"Oh no," said Otto, clamping his hand to his mouth, *"we forgot!"*

"Well," I told them, *"you will just jolly well get back up there and put that right!"* They didn't go!

Could this be my first dissenter?

I was in despair when I got comments from Tony (left), a saxophonist in The Old Green River jazz band, and his friend Duncan. Tony said *"I think there is a myth about the mountain – the highest point in Great Britain and that's why people climb it – because it's not beautiful – it's barren isn't it?"*

I wasn't liking what I was hearing – but wait...

"But it lifts you into a realm of beauty." Yeh man – Way to go!

Tony plays "You ain't nothin' but a Hound Dog" on his sax as Mike Davies "leads" us out of the park in the same fashion as Duncan MacIntyre forty years previously!

43

Molly is a black shadow..

...in the afternoon sun as her master and mistress make their way up. They are Robert and "Wills" from England.

Barney the Sprightly Springer...

...ten years old, is on his way down. He hails from Doncaster with his owners, Pete and Julie. They had enjoyed the views up until they disappeared into the mist near the top. Julie was particularly proud to have made it, as she is an asthma sufferer and had left her puffer at home. As Pete said *"you can't get any air purer than this, can you?"*

"We are very proud of ourselves..."

Loch Linnhe

Loch Eil

Pulp Mill

...say Fay and her sister from Perth doing the climb for breast cancer and for underprivileged children who might never get a chance to do something like this themselves. *"We could never have believed that we could do this climb, but we have done it and we are so proud of ourselves, aren't we? Completely exhilarated. Cameron MacNeish is talking out of his hat! We think it's brilliant! I would prefer to think of it as Heaven rather than Hell!"*

"Heaven" and "Venomous one" are the two opposing translations of "Nevis". The poet, John Keats wound the names into a sonnet after his climb of The Ben on 2nd of August, 1818 – *"Mankind do know of Hell"... "Mankind can tell of Heaven."* He had a misty day! I go along with the girls with Heaven! However, many others feel the Pony Track is a long boring plod not seeing the mountain at its best – too populous in the height of

summer, endless zigzags, nearly always in the mist and they describe the Tourist Track as the nasty alternative meaning – pure hell! But not us! Every inch of that path has its own memory for me in my association with The Ben since 1968 and you will be hearing them all before the end of the book!

The fetching hats were extremely useful higher up in the clouds – you just followed the tinkling of the bells!

So, ladies, we're proud of you too, for raising money for such worthy causes. Everyone who does these sponsored events is a star, but often you get TV stars on The Ben and this made it an even more extra-special day in the life of Tracy MacGillivray when she met Trudie Goodwin who plays Sgt. June Ackland in "The Bill" – read on...

Whilst proceeding in an upwardly direction

Photo courtesy of Iain Ferguson

Sgt. June Ackland of "The Bill" met Tracy MacGillivray who was on her way down The Ben. Tracy was making her dreams come true. She lives at Banavie and had looked out of her window everyday at the top of The Ben (when visible!), wishing she could climb it. Tracy has been paralysed for 17 years following a car crash. Her wish was granted when she was whisked up to the top in a helicopter and delivered to the safe hands of – no, not Big Kenny Campbell of piano, organ and beer barrel fame - but Nevis Guide, Mick Tighe. Tracy was soon under way on a "Joulette", a one wheeled stretcher, perhaps passing some of the runners on the way down as it was the same day as the race! Tracy was being sponsored for spinal research and Trudie Goodwin, TV star of the police drama, was fundraising for the National Osteoporosis Society in memory of her mum, who'd been a sufferer. Cancer Research was to the fore on The Ben also that week, as Chris from Blackpool and in the RAF was staying five days with his collecting tin. Chris had coined a new weather phenomenon – "Clizzle"- a cross between cloud and drizzle, where "it turns nineteen corners then lands on something making it wet!" It reminded me of the weather condition that the Observers encountered, which they called "Silver Thaw" – rain falling when the temperature was below freezing point, coating everything with a film of ice. For one night Chris had neighbours! A German couple, Linda and Stefan. They had hoped for a bit less rocks and a bit more warmth but were well provided for with "noodles". It was amusing that Chris's support team at ground level were telling people to take him water and Mars bars – before he could get word down for them to stop, he had a pyramid of them and his rucksac was going to weigh about 50 pounds more to carry down!

Stanislov, lover of tourism,...

...was on his first visit to Scotland and on a coach tour from The Czech Republic to the Outer Isles. He pointed down to his bus way below. You can just spot it to the left of the Youth Hostel with a magnifying glass!

Also on their way down were Jim and his daughter Jenny – all the way from Down Under. It was their first visit and Jim's verdict was *"A wonderful feeling getting there. The views on the way up are just magnificent. It's a challenge and it is great to see so many people doing it."*

Jenny said, *"it makes you know you're alive."*

Jim has climbed the highest points in four of the Australian States but says that the Aborigines don't like people to climb Ayers Rock.

I'd come upon Dave (bottom left) earlier when he was enquiring of Stanislov just how much further it was to the top. Sad to say he'd many a zig and many a zag to go before striding the summit stones. He made me laugh by asking if there was a closing time! He declined to go into the photo with Stanislov, saying he was not yet worthy! Well he certainly proved he was, with his determination to get to the top, click clicking away with his stick as he went steadily up and he agreed to "strike a pose" near the summit. Originally from Scotland, he moved to Maidstone when aged 18. He told me he was going to have words with his brother for telling him it was easy!

Photo courtesy of Roberto Matassa

The Sun has got his hat on

Photo courtesy of Alex Gillespie

Good weather for "Freeing Willie"...

...on Christiana's tee shirt! Mum and dad Carl are on the "Resting Stones" with son Paul. At 3,000 feet, this is a common turning back spot just before entering the zag of the 2nd Zigzag, but take heart, for the arms of the zigzags get shorter from here-on-in. The family is from Poole and has Scottish Country Dancing as their hobby - there is a dance called Pelorus Jack, about a dolphin exchanging the lead with a boat. The trio was pausing here to take a photo as the mists had lifted for a moment, only to return – no cries of **"Hip-hip-hip-hooray"** like the last page! The sight of the "Captain Scott" (captured so beautifully by Roberto Matassa in the

Photo courtesy of Royal Scottish Geographical society

morning with the sun rising over the shoulder of The Ben, and again in the evening by Alex Gillespie with the sun setting in the west) would have sparked off many memories for these Observers - W.S. Bruce, D.W. (Eddie the Eagle) Wilton and R.C. Mossman. They were off on the "Scotia Antarctic Expedition" with the first mentioned as leader. To commemorate the hundredth anniversary of the event a book of dances was published in 2002 and "Bruce's Men" (gathered above) is one of them. Another dance (as you can see from the photo over on the right...) is called "The Piper and the Penguin". I can just picture ex-Observatory staff regaling their shipmates with tales of their life in Britain's highest Outpost - "D.W." especially, as he had attempted the first ever ski jump on Ben

Nevis – launching out over McLean's Steep and braining himself in the process! Luckily another person was there to spot his legs sticking out of the snow! One thing William Bruce could recount, as the ship sailed south, was the time they opened the door of the Observatory and a fox was standing there! Runners going up The Ben in the quiet of the evening have spotted a couple of shy pine martens on the summit. My favourite animal story on The Ben is of the badger that fell over the cliff and rolled down "Green Gully" which fortunately was full of snow. At the bottom the badger shook itself, then tried to climb back up!

There have been 4 ships called Ben Nevis in the Ben Line and the first one, pictured  on this box of matches, was in service from 1928 – 1941 when it was captured off Hong Kong during the war and renamed "Gyokuyo Maru". The ill-fated ship lasted 2 more years before being on the receiving end of an American torpedo.

Photo courtesy of Royal Scottish Geographical society

Chapter 5
YOU NOW HAVE "MUNRO" STATUS
THE MAGICAL HEIGHT OF 3,000
3,000ft to 4,000ft

Photo courtesy of Scottish Mountaineering Club

SIR HUGH Munro (background photo) gave his name to the famous Munro's Tables, the list of hills over 3,000ft and the Rev.A.E.Robertson (on the right) was the first person to climb them all, finishing his last one after ten years in 1901. No one repeated that for 20 years! Then along came a real character called Ronnie Burn (another minister), who completed the round plus all the separate tops. In Betty Allan's excellent book "Burn on the Hill" she describes wonderfully the way he existed on only a five-day-old cheese sandwich! In the photo with her is Fr. Anthony Ross, a companion of Ronnie's when a young man. Jimmy Allan wrote in my copy of the book how his late wife Betty had written it with love and affection and how she had so admired the spirit in which Ronnie tackled the hills. Jimmy is a "weel kent" figure in the Old Time Dancing circles.

Photo courtesy of SMC

Photo courtesy of Jimmy Allan

Dramatic pause as Frank's story unfolds!

"I would just like to say......that it looked easy from the ground. ....I looked up and said......there's the top!......But when you start walking every corner just seems to go on and on. ....Eventually 100 metres to go......and I must reach the top." I'd met Frank and Sally from Bedford earlier on, on their way up at the end of the zig part of the 3rd Zigzag. They'd gone on a false trail. Instead of turning the corner in the Pony Track, they'd gone straight on up which isn't funny so close to Five Finger Gully! They sensibly turned back when the path ended. So on my way down I got a group to point out the only true way! Ursula and Hans are from Austria and Arne (on the right) from England. Arne shared his friends' views that it was impressive and that he ought to come more often to Ben Nevis and the Highlands. When you reach here, imagine them blocking your path and "hang a left".

Here comes "Dodger" heading down from "Black Rock"

It is purely coincidental that he should be on a training session after the announcement at the 2003 race prizegiving that a bonus of £1000 would be given to the first to beat the men's and ladies' records which have stood for 20 years at **1hr 25mins 34secs and 1hr 43mins 25secs** respectively! Both records were set in 1984 and the two runners were later to become husband and wife, Kenny Stuart and Pauline Haworth of Keswick AC. Davy Rodgers, remember, is a three times Ben Nevis Race winner and looks poised to knock off those elusive minutes for the bounty. He has already been under the magical figure of 1hr 30mins for The Ben. He was 7th in 2003 and you can see his clutch of trophies for that day in John MacRae's "A Verse on The Ben" page. At the time of the above photo in September 2003, Davy had come a very good 32nd in the World Trophy in Alaska.

Davy's "wee" brother, Billy, on the left of the picture with Billy Brooks and their collection of Ben Nevis trophies, looked set for victory in place of Davy who was at the World Championships in France in 1993. Billy was third at the top and then... "It was a nightmare, I just died after the summit and couldn't give any more.", finishing 12th but was 4th the next year in 1hr 33mins 12secs. Billy Brooks was 48th - just pipped by brother Graham!

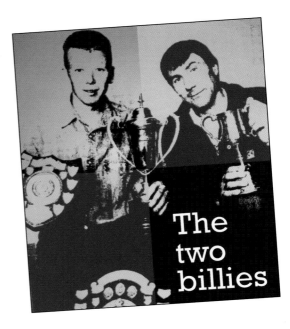

The two billies

Ship-shape

This team from Bristol managed to remain fashionable and cheery, even after a bit of a misunderstanding when they'd asked someone for directions lower down. When I met them, they had just emerged, slightly traumatised, from the way the runners come – straight up the Red Burn! Rather than asking again for the way to get to the top, their leader had gone on ahead to spy out the land and to ensure they were still on Ben Nevis! All agreed that the views were stunning and it was a great sense of achievement to be up there. Fran, Paul, Paul and Neil are from Bristol and Sarah in front is from over the Severn from them in Wales. They'd just come up the very prominent and tempting looking rib shaped path, which you see on the right of the photo (left). **Don't yield to that temptation** on your way down - for it soon peters out into a broken, rocky, near vertical hell. It is, as I said to the Bristol ones, the way the runners come up and go down! I asked Robert (left) from Quebec as he walked past to point out the true way down the Pony Track. Robert said his climb was "just fabulous!"

And here on the right is Kate, the Bristol team leader, who'd gone on ahead to find the route. She had a request for the summit – to have a new knee fitted for getting back down! She had hurt her knee earlier in their holiday, but was wearing a brave smile for her troops.

James' "See you Jimmy" hat...

...ought to have been called "don't see you" on a misty day like this. You can even buy a postcard of Ben Nevis in the mist in the shops!

Remaining very cheery despite the weather, these lads from Edwinstowe, Nottingham, had been busy over the last four days. James, with friends Chris, Duncan and Tom, had gone from Land's End to John o' Groats climbing Snowdon and Scafell Pike on the way. This was them finishing on The Ben. They felt Scafell was a harder climb technically, but that for The Ben endurance was the name of the game.

The weather was similarly "yuck" for these Liverpuddlian pals (pictured below) and they were just as cheery... They treated me to a rendition of *"Above us only sky"* and had been surprised by the sight of Chris the RAF man camping at the top, Jim (on the right) thinking that Chris was up there selling "The Big Issue"!

Gemma with her clipboard...

...is doing a survey for her A level Geography on the tourist impact on Ben Nevis. She and her dad are from Wooton Bassett near Swindon and had picked a nice day to go up – that little mist in the photo had just blown in and blew out just as quickly.

People often stand and stare at this point where Gemma is (the distinctive little round shelter of rocks), wondering which path to take. The answer is either one, as explained on the next page.

Below is a photo of Klaus, who had continued straight on the Pony Track and is admiring the view at the 4,000ft mark, out beyond the head of Loch Eil to the two Cuillins – the Cuillin of Rum and the Cuillin of Skye, little clumps of mountains hidden in the haze. Klaus from Canada is a long distance walker, but was kind of dreading the descent as he has pins in his knees following a skiing accident where he nobly elected to hit the only tree on the piste rather than run someone over!

Shortcuts - to be or not to be

The policy for shortcutting is often laid down by the team leader setting out the rules before you start. In the case of Simon (in the white shirt and raring to go) the rule about the party remaining together had to be flexed as the rest of his companions were being driven mad trying to hold him on a leash! A runner on a coach holiday with non-runners! So he was allowed to go on ahead, but only on the strictest instructions that he never ever under any circumstances took a shortcut. Simon slowed down just long enough for me to get a picture of him alongside Andy from Belgium. Andy was heading up at a more measured pace with the heavy pack!

The best advice about the shortcuts comes from the Ranger Service:

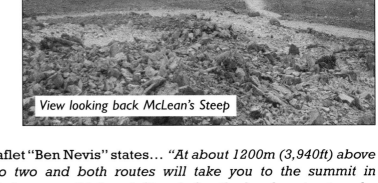

View looking back McLean's Steep

BEFORE HALFWAY

Melantee 1st Zigzag	No shortcutting!
Melantee 2nd Zigzag	No shortcutting!
Zigzag to Halfway Loch	No shortcutting!

AFTER HALFWAY

1st Zigzag	No shortcutting!
2nd Zigzag	No shortcutting!
3rd Zigzag	No shortcutting!
4th Zigzag	No shortcutting!

5th Zigzag   Ranger Service leaflet "Ben Nevis" states... *"At about 1200m (3,940ft) above sea level the track flattens out. It splits into two and both routes will take you to the summit in approximately 30 minutes. The last steep rise is known as 'McLean's Steep' after the local contractor who built the Observatory. The path then traverses across the plateau close to the hazardous edge of Tower Gully and Gardyloo Gully finally turning in a north-easterly direction for approximately 150m to the summit cairn.* **(1343m, 4406ft) (4 hours from start)"**

The Five Zigzags

Here comes Jamie showing just what "true grit" means and at the same time making **£15,000** for charity as he climbs The Ben in June 2000. Just a year and a half earlier, Jamie Andrew had had to have his frost-bitten arms and legs cut off below the elbows and knees after an horrific ordeal on "Les Droites" in the Alps. I think every single person in the large audience at Jamie's talk at the Annual Fort William Mountain Festival in February '04, came away totally inspired! What laughter he caused when he showed a slide of a Greek God who'd had similar amputations! He demonstrated how he masters drinking a "pint", but says that it is a thing that requires constant practice! He also described how he arrived up on the summit of The Ben and the RAF personnel accompanying him said they had a nice surprise for him...

What a "feet"!

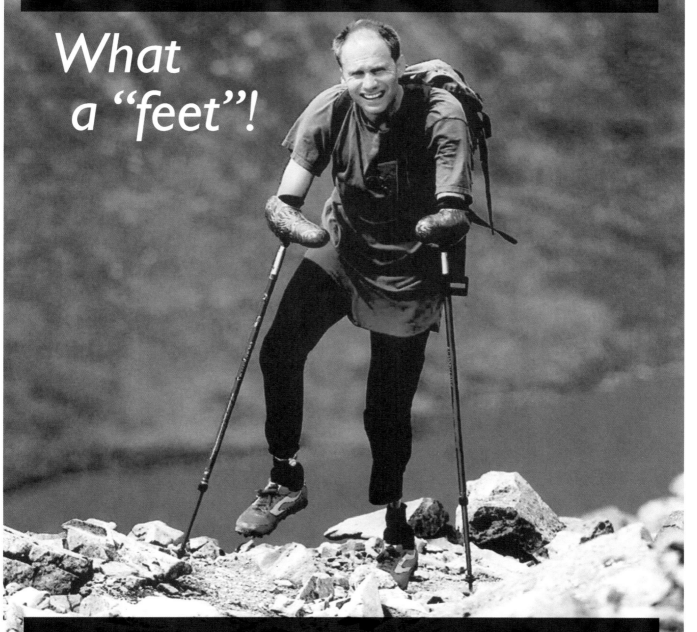

The surprise was in the shape of a helicopter, which whisked Jamie off on a breathtaking tour of all the neuks and crannies of The Ben. *"Just outside 'the Crofters' would be lovely."* Jamie suggested hopefully to the pilot, but the RAF has too many scruples and he was deposited back on the summit!

Photo courtesy of Jamie

Chapter 6
WELCOME TO THE UPPER REACHES
4,000ft to 4,406ft

Only half an hour to go

Jade and Gary from Cheshire

A S WE get higher up The Ben, so we reach the first page with the out of season warning signs for the photo - the snow zone layer! We all joke about Eddie's non PC approach to clothing and footwear but cheeky young Wendy Dodds from Clayton-le-Moors Harriers has a story of Eddie wearing shoes to an event that even predated his famous *"Green Flash"*...

"- black plimsolls that looked suspiciously like those all older people will have purchased from the well-known High Street shop beginning with W for their school P.E.." Wendy had been describing a run round *"Tranter's Round"* and went on to say that she ended up with sore knees with her *"trainers of good repute"* whereas Eddie had no ill effects!

Leading the way

Getting a "Buzz"...

...from playing in his first snow is James's Sheltie. Buzz was having a whale of a time chasing snowballs until, like all pups, it was time for a nap – on James's shoulders! James had driven up from Bristol on a few days' holiday from his job as a petrol tanker driver. He spoke fondly of his previous dog, Ricky, who went up The Ben when aged fourteen.

Coming from Middlesborough are Michael and Sharon

Michael knows The Ben well as he organises long events in the "fells". The sky is blue, but the air is perishing and making you realise that winter draws on! Changing the clocks at the end of October may be all right for an extra hour in bed, but it means less daylight for up and down The Ben!

Frank and his son Joseph come striding down past the silver birches, whose leaves are turning to gold. They'd come up from Crail in Fife to climb The Ben during the October "tattie howkin' (potato picking) holidays". Another Scottish expression is "Gardyloo!" which they used to shout in the old days of Edinburgh tenements when about to throw a pailful of slops into the street below. Frank and Joseph had been fascinated with the gullies at the summit, the one nearest the Observatory being called Gardyloo Gully as that is where they used to "slop out" – unless in a south wind where they just threw it up in the air (keeping tight hold of the bucket!) and the wind did the rest! It was, however, a dangerous job and a complex apparatus was set up…

The trio on bucket duty roped together and anchored themselves in the snow as the leader went over onto the gantry. An Observer's ski had slid over the edge one-day and its owner got the others to lower him to the ledge where it lay about 25 yards down. When it came to pulling him up, the rope cut into the cornice and jammed and they all began to freeze. The desperate situation was resolved when who should arrive on the scene but a party from the Scottish Mountaineering Club and they soon had him whisked up. When rock climbers started exploring The Ben they tended to keep away from directly below the Observatory as they only wore flat caps! Especially when you read about rocks being rolled over for fun! In a chapter headed

Photo courtesy of Royal Meterological Society

"Pastimes" in his book "Twenty Years on Ben Nevis", William Kilgour describes starting huge avalanches by easing rocks up to half a ton over the edge to listen and watch as the earth shook! He says, *"the boom and thunder was comparable to a battery of artillery in action!"* Some brave (?) souls even went down into the Coire Leis valley below the cliffs and took cover before the cannonade commenced, the better to feel the "nuance"! Imagine the Observers' surprise if they could have seen the low flying aircraft of our time on the other side of the mountain! The planes will come jetting past Melantee matching *"the boom and thunder"* and disappear over the Peat Track from Glen Nevis with a roar that bounces from hill to hill long after the plane has gone. Just after I'd spoken to Frank and Joseph, I was walking down the road from Achintee thinking how good a photo of a plane would be. Lo and behold, a jet was coming straight for me...

Hastily I drew my camera, undoing it from all its protective cases and swivelled round to take the shot of the century. Too little and too late! The pilot would have been landing in Leuchars by then! So I'll borrow one from "clipart"...

When Tracy undid her anorak...

...it was to reveal the legend "LOCHABER PEOPLES MARATHON"! She and her dad are from Irvine and on holiday in a motorhome with the three kids. The pair do sponsored runs for Cancer Research as well as going along to Scottish Country Dancing. Visitors to Fort William are very welcome to come along to the Kilmallie class - but be prepared to be dragged up to take part!). It's a very nice way to relax after The Ben! There will be a poster in the town centre.

The Lochaber Peoples Marathon, pictured here with the runners going out Locheilside, was Eddie's brain child and Eddie was there himself in the pack. A loud voice rang out from the back *"Don't go up The Ben, Eddie!"* One year, staggering over the finishing line after the 26 odd miles, I hung round Jane's neck and Eddie quipped *"That's enough of that now!"*

SCOTTISH COUNTRY DANCING
in
KILMALLIE HALL, CORPACH
8.00-10.00p.m
every TUESDAY
in JULY and AUGUST
Adults: £1.50
Children: £1.00

Photo courtesy of Scotland's Runner

The happy group at the gully...

...surprised me when Yun (2nd from right) said he hated me! We had been talking earlier lower down The Ben and I'd taken his and his friend Andree's photo with the halfway loch in the background. Yun had told me he was from Beijing and was studying "Risk Management" in London. Andree had said he was from Germany and had climbed Snowdon but it had been wet in Wales, hence the reason he had brought so many clothes. I had said cheerio and set off on up, little

knowing that they'd sort of extended themselves in trying to keep up! They should have commandeered some of the dogs on The Ben and made a team. They could have had one each of these Westies! The dogs belong to the Jones's from Wiltshire. My own dog is a retired sheep dog called "Tot" and if I'd taken her up The Ben on that particular day she'd have needed therapy as they were gathering the sheep at Achintee! Here she is pictured safely at home with Jane.

"Beautiful views but a hard slog."

So said Tom and Sarah from Manchester. They added that it was well worth it but could have done with more water on a lovely hot day. With a flourish, I brought out a bottle of Spar's finest. "Oh! How much?" they asked, looking longingly.

"A present from Scotland" I said, not letting on that it was the free part of "buy one, get one free"! The last water on the way up the Pony Track is this spring (below) on the zig part of the third zigzag. It runs out of the rock, which almost looks sculpted. It is just a dribble in hot weather. The spring at which Clement Wragge took his 08.15 and 10.50 readings is higher up, but is not on the path. That spring, Buchan's Well, is over in the rocky screes of the Red Burn – out of bounds! The Buchan mentioned was Alexander Buchan, Secretary of the Scottish Meteorological Society during the life of the Observatory. Most people vaguely remember something about "Buchan's Cold Spells" whenever it gets unusually chilly. In fact, such notice was taken of these spells that Parliament's idea to have an annual fixed date for the Easter holiday weekend was scuppered when someone said it coincided with a "Cold Spell"! Alexander Buchan himself kept telling folk that these spells were purely local records kept of weather in Edinburgh and not general – but no one listened. He would have preferred to be correctly given his place in history as the father of the isobars we see on TV telling us how windy it is going to be. The Observers and the hotel staff used a well near the summit, but it too dried up in summer. You can still see the wooden tank if you follow the little path behind the Observatory that the summit dwellers did tread...

Well travelled!

If you managed to find the dinky little zigzags, which take you down to "Wragge's Well", you will find the spring and the water tank (now a dried out wooden box), which was brought from the war zone in the Sudan right up to the top of The Ben. On a fine day you can have a fabulous view of the Steall waterfall.

Come on a misty day and you can feel the atmospherics of the long gone hotel staff and Observers dipping in their buckets!

Congratulations
on the reaching the summit !

What a moment!

You too will savour the elation that is written all over Tordis's face when you reach the top!

Tordis is in the 1984 Ben Nevis Race and is meeting up with hubby, Ian Donaldson, who's in his usual marshalling place atop The Ben.

Their daughter Emmy lent me her favourite photo of them and said that looking at it again has inspired her to enter the race herself!

Here we are at 4,406 feet!

I hope you arrive here on a good day and have a chance to look around the Observatory ruins and get your photo taken after clambering up to the Trig Point – I'm sure someone will oblige you with your camera, but be warned when they say "back a bit!"

Snow will linger on until June on the top, then it should clear until the end of September. Notice the change around of furniture on the top!

To mark the *100th* anniversary

of the opening of the Observatory, the Royal Meterological Society went up re-enacting a typical day in the life of Clement Wragge (remember that meant a 4°° am start – but the 75 who went were allowed an extra hour in bed going at 5°°!). Wind speed on the right is just being read from the anemometer but in the days of the Observatory the top of the wind scale was taken as when the roof would be blown off!

Mick Tighe, the mountain guide, led the party up on 25th June 1983, rather than chance the weather of the actual anniversary in October. Mick in fact returned to the summit on the 17th October to hold a week long course of living on the summit and taking weather readings – **dig the weather!** I attended the anniversary climb but not the course!

Alex Gillespie's photo shows Jim Watson of the Met Office sending in a weather report – snow showers!

Britain's highest couple...

...is Jan and Juliann who climbed up in three and a half hours. They found the going hard, but then they mustn't have rested much on the way up. At the top they admired the view with the cone of Schiehallion, 36 miles away. Perhaps at that very moment someone was on the top down there, looking back at The Ben – maybe the paparazzi with their huge lenses watching for Lord and Lady Archer, who climbed The Ben when staying at Inverlochy Castle!

Sona

Photo courtesy of Iain Thomson

Iain Thomspon

Becky   Tot

"Good Collie Miss Mollie"

Iain moved to Fort William from Ayrshire and is well known for his books, especially "The Black Cloud" (left), which features the accident on The Ben in 1934 when one of the leading climbers of the era, Maurice Linnell, was killed.

Iain's dog Sona is pictured on the trig point when she was 3 years old in 1985 – "Top dog" indeed! Sona means "happy". Iain's present dog, Becky, is 10 and has many Munros under her collar, the previous day they'd been up on the hills on the other side of Glen Nevis. Before meeting Iain and Becky, Tot and I met another collie down at Achintee - her master was Ian McColl (below), the Glen Nevis shepherd who knew Tot's previous owner, Colin MacGregor from Lochearnhead. In the leaflet, "Ben Nevis", Ian says, *"On the lower path you will walk through Achintee Grazings which are an important part of my working life in the Glen and reflect a life time commitment to this hill land. Please respect this."*

More collie "tails"

An Observer was making his way up The Ben to report for duty when a collie followed him. He ordered it home, but it kept returning – fortunately for the Observer because he slipped on ice in the Red Burn screes and the dog latched its teeth into the man's coat to save him.

A nice little win on the lottery...

...would pay for a new bronze chart for the indicator, but for so vast a view, you would need something the size of a dinner table for all the info... and who will volunteer to carry that up? The indicator hasn't aged since my dancing friend Helma's photo of her mum and dad, Helma and Lawrie on their honeymoon in 1935.

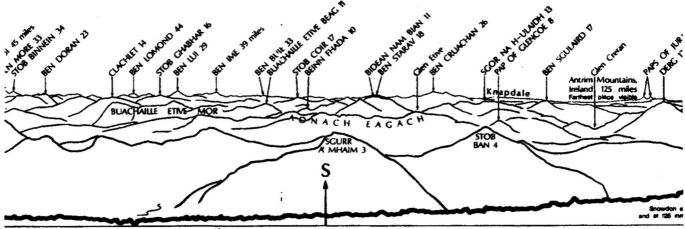

The chart above was published in 1895 by James E. Shearer, who drew up the panorama on the summit in what must have been a very demanding project. The chart was lent to Chris Jesty who made this edition in 1977, as he says "without having to leave my desk"! The donor was none other than Alf Wainwright, MBE, whose sketches of the hills are legendary. The chart shows the furthest away point visible at 125 miles – the Antrim Mountains.

Alas there had been no horizon for Osertz and Sergio on their visit to the summit, but they weren't downhearted as they made their way down from the mist further up. They are from the Basque region of Spain and Majorca respectively. A pity there was no grand vista for them, in particular Osertz, because he informed me that his name means "Horizon"!

68

Party time at the top!

Muriel Gray (top right) added a real splash of colour to the summit when she threw a party complete with sit down banquet with chefs from the Dunblane Hydro preparing the meal. The Llamas were so pleased that they weren't the day's "special"! One of the Llamas decided it didn't want to carry its panniers, so sat down and refused to budge, until George Bruce (right) kindly took its packs off and added them to his own! More of George's exploits follow on the next page...

Photos courtesy of Ian Donaldson and George Bruce

Left: *Muriel seems to be asking just who is going to clean up this little lot?*

Right: *Enter the 4-legged Hoover, Tot! - being held back by Peter and Emilie from near Amsterdam. Peter had often come to Scotland in his days of playing the bagpipes.*

There seems to be some dispute here as to who saw the 10p first!

But really of course there is no contest because George is from Aberdeen! Prince Charles was spending a day with the Lochaber Mountain Rescue in August 1987. George Bruce, the one on the receiving end of the pointing ice axe, lent me his fabulous album of Ben Nevis memories and it reads like a "who's who" of summit celebrities...

George says:-
"A man walked up backwards using mirrors"

George says:-
"A man in a rhinoceros suit was saving the white rhino"

George says:-
"A large party of paraplegics made their way up on padded bums"

George says:-
"During one rescue, 22 of the team slept in the shelter at the top!"

William Hague and wife Ffion on the top with George Bruce in April 2000. Ffion's comment was "I've climbed Snowdon before, but didn't realise how hard it would be to get up and down Ben Nevis!" She also said that William had often to be "reined in" for going off at 100mph! Charlie's axe in the top photo will serve us as the out of season warning. Another Charlie was taken up by George – Charlie Dymock, the TV gardener (left) – to look for the £1 coin George had dropped earlier in the week!

A *red letter* day for the Ben

The 1st October 2003 was a really beautiful day and an important one for Ben Nevis – "monumental" in fact! On their way up the mountain was a party from "Historic Scotland", coming to view the ruins of the Observatory to decide whether to make them a National Monument or raze them to the ground. They came, they saw and they said "Yes!" Who could have done other than "save save save" on a day like this? It also avoided the problem of how to get a bulldozer up! This new status will ensure that work can be done to stabilise the ruins and avoid them degenerating any further. It would have been really tough luck on a visitor if they'd come all the way from the other side of the world to climb The Ben just to have the old walls fall on them while they had their picnic!

There is no intention, though, that the Observatory would ever be rebuilt. Various fires throughout the long time it's remained empty and the filling up each winter with snow rotting the timbers have seen to that. On the right is how the building looked in the 1930s (Helma again with two other climbers) when thought was given to reopen it for the series of International Polar Years. James Miller, ex-Observatory Cook and general factotum, was raring to go although at that time now in his seventies! He had kept open the Observatory Hotel until its closure in 1916. William Kilgour himself must have thought that his lifelong dream of seeing the Observatory back in use was about to come true – imagine how this must have fired his enthusiasm until his death in 1932. But it was just a dream. It would have taken too much to redo the sodden timbers and make good the road and bridges to get the materials up. It was in the fifties that the old Observatory building really became irreparable – the lead roof upon which the Observers would lie and sunbathe was surreptitiously stripped off to be sold to finance climbing expeditions!

In the photo above, Ken MacTaggart from Inverness is taking notes of the memorials on the cairn for an article on The Ben for an American magazine "Scottish Life". He required pictures with no snow and judged it perfectly as a few days later, as you will see in the "Precious moments" page, the top half of the mountain took on its winter mantle of snow.

Photo courtesy of Helma Reynolds (Jnr)

The story of the lead from the roof made me laugh fit to bust! One climber described cutting up the lead into strips then, seeing some tourists approaching the summit, hastily packed the rolled up lead into his rucksack and set off down the Pony Track whistling nonchalantly and wishing the visitors a good day.

This was fine and dandy for all of one hundred yards then he sank to his knees under the weight! A nice little bounty awaits someone to this day, as the poor climber managed to struggle to halfway with his booty, then he built a cairn round it, intending to return but never did. The late Brian Kearney said bits of lead lay abandoned in the Red Burn screes as he trained in the '50s.

Wm Kilgour (left hand side of the above picture with some visitors) and the Penicuik Rover Scouts both had the same view of the lead roof for sun bathing...

"In the height of summer, when, for weeks at a stretch, the sun temperature mounted to 130°, it was difficult to shake off an inherent feeling of lassitude. Rambles of exploration were then at a discount – far more satisfying was it to lounge on the Observatory roof, though, even in this, one had to be careful, if respect were to be paid to the nether extremities, for, so hot did the lead become with the sun's rays, that it occasionally proved unbearable to the touch."

(From "Twenty Years on Ben Nevis")

*"In the sun's golden rays let me loll and laze
Till my skin is red and flaking,
On my back let me lie, till my belly will fry*

*Two eggs
and a rasher of bacon!"*

(From the Rovers!)

Mr *Phin* and his *party...*

...must have had some very funny looks if this tea towel is a true likeness! Some of the ladies are real dishes!

The highest spot in the land is the focal point for many monuments and momentoes, although not many are funny like this one (right). Some are very sad, like one message for a lost love said, *"This is as near as I can get to you for now."*

On Captain Pip's visit to the summit, she said she was humbled by so many wonderful memorials, especially some to forces personnel. When Cap'n Pip read one memorial to a very young girl who'd been climbing The Ben since she was four years old, she said, *"I take my beret off to her!*

By day - 2003

Photos courtesy of Ken MacTaggart

By night - 1903

Here are two of the views that Ken took whilst on the top for inclusion in his "Scottish Life" article and I can imagine the readers thrilling at the dizzy drops! Top photo is looking across Gardyloo Gully and below right is Tower Gully

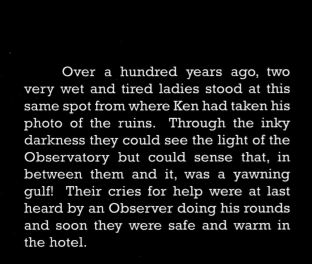

Over a hundred years ago, two very wet and tired ladies stood at this same spot from where Ken had taken his photo of the ruins. Through the inky darkness they could see the light of the Observatory but could sense that, in between them and it, was a yawning gulf! Their cries for help were at last heard by an Observer doing his rounds and soon they were safe and warm in the hotel.

Precious moments...

...on a mountain of two halves, as Jim and I were recalling Precious Mackenzie the weight lifter. At the height of his fitness for the clean and jerk sport, Jim had done The Ben in three and a half hours. He said it was a sight to see - him and his three foster sons running down, with him weighing sixteen stone! That solves a twentyfive year old riddle for the seismologists about the bumpity bump bumps on the chart! Today, however, Jim and Dawn were staying below whilst the two girls, Yvonne and Kelly, went up into the snow. Jim said in the three times he'd been up, he'd never had a view beyond halfway but that the girls were going to be lucky. Not! Here the pair are – before and after!

Evening draws on as homeward they tread.

"The Arête" looking towards The Ben

Photo courtesy of Moira Burks, pictured with son Carl, taken by her late husband Alver.

Robert here, from Midcalder, had had a big day! He had left at 7am and had climbed Carn Mòr Dearg, The Ben's neighbour. It is well named "Dearg" because that is Gaelic for red and that is exactly how it looks when you look down on it from the summit of The Ben. You pronounce it Carn More Jerrag. It is joined to The Ben by a narrow ridge called "The Arête". It's not really for your everyday Ben Path climber like ourselves! It requires a good head for heights and you should read Muriel Gray's sidesplitting description of it in *"The First Fifty"* before you contemplate it! Years ago, I found a rusty old bit of an ice axe below the ridge and was remembering it when The Arête was very much in the news recently. A member of a long ago school party suddenly claimed, after 50 years, that their teacher had been shoved to his death off the edge of the ridge! The true story was that he had fallen trying to retrieve an ice axe. Because this happened so long ago, enquiries took time to trace the remaining people on the trip, but those contacted unanimously said how well loved the teacher was, so no way was he pushed!

Adrienne and John (below) from Lancashire had done the same route as Robert via the summit of Carn Mòr Dearg. They are keen Munroists and it was a real bonus to have this fantastic view from the top. They don't look as if they would fall out, but be warned if your loved-one suggests doing The Arête after taking out a whacking big insurance policy on your life! While I was speaking to them, the winners from the Three Peaks' Yacht Race came trotting up to the trig point – their boat was called the "Spirit of Barmouth" and they were about 6 hours ahead of their rivals. The TV film crew that had followed them throughout, up Snowdon and Scafell Pike and the sea journey in between, said it was so calm that the mighty Corryvreckan whirlpool off the island of Jura was just a few bubbles. The Paps of Jura can sometimes be seen from the top - 77 miles away.

Chapter 7
RACES, RUNNERS AND RECORDS

THE FELL RUNNER
SUMMER 1979

25p

Cover courtesy of The Fellrunner and here is what they say... "The popular husband and wife fell running team of Anne and Pete Bland shown here completing the 1978 Peebles Karrimor mountain marathon. They finished 33rd in the Elite class, the first mixed pair (Anne making history as the first Elite lady to finish). Photo by courtesy of Gordon Petrie."

NO BEN Nevis Race is complete without runners looking round Pete's van – especially after the race if the screes have taken their toll on your equipment! Pete Bland has a long history of fell running, having come from the professional side in the Lake District and captaining the English International Team.

Here he is with wife Anne on the cover of the "Fell Runners' Association" magazine - eagerly awaited three times a year! They are finishing just a hundred yards from my door in Peebles in the 1978 Karrimor 2 day race. Also pairing up in that event were Chris Brasher, another boot designer, and John Disley.

Pete rates 1973, the same as me, as his best Ben Nevis Race and you will see the Bland family name well to the fore in the Ben Nevis Race results over the years - Billy winning in 1978 and his nephew Gavin in 92' and '97.

Anne and Pete are well worthy choices to lead off the chapter on Races, runners and records.

The Racing Section...

In 1980 Fort William was all of a flutter when "Ben Nevis" won the Grand National at 40/1.

"Ben Nevis" may have survived the rigours of "Becher's Brook", but not poor Bob... I met him halfway up the "Field of Cairns" where you can see the snowbank of the (almost) Eternal Snows in the background dwindling away in the warm sunshine and he kept me amused for about half an hour with his tales of misadventure. He really deserves a book of his own! Bob was on a Land's End to John o' Groats walk for Yorkhill Children's Hospital and had come up The Ben on his way north. Becher's Brook, for those who haven't heard of the infamous fence in the Grand National, is normal on the side the horses approach, then there is an unexpected drop on the other side! This is exactly what Bob discovered when he stepped over a low wall in the dark to kip down for the night in a Taunton park! He finished up with an ankle the size of a balloon after a twenty foot fall! He tried to continue his walk in the hope it would get better, but eventually had to go to hospital. It was found that nothing was broken, but in the meantime one of his boots had been stolen! Bob was given a replacement at a church – a sandal! His sponsors kindly donated him another pair, which he is proudly showing off.

"Eddie"
by Graham Brooks

Photo courtesy of Roger Boswell

We all knew Eddie Campbell, that familiar figure with the white beard and friendly face, who could be seen almost daily running along the footpaths of Fort William and Glen Nevis. Dressed in tee shirt and shorts and clutching a handkerchief to mop his brow, this legendary Ben Nevis runner was an accepted part of everyday life in Lochaber. A modest man who lived life to the full and enjoyed the simple things that God gave him – his loving family and the fresh air and mountains.

In recent years he was known as "Old Eddie". Eddie was never really old. When you spoke with him, you could see the sparkle in his eye and his tremendous energy.

Eddie did not look for fame or fortune and his forty-four Ben Nevis Races were not run for winner's glory, although he had tasted this three times when he was a young man. Indeed, even when he had reached the age of fifty, he was still breaking the two-hour barrier. At the annual Cow Hill Race Eddie would be standing on the summit every year. His words of encouragement, "Keep the trot going, boys," always seemed to give the runners that little extra incentive to keep going.

I once mentioned to Eddie that I had great difficulty in walking downstairs due to soreness in my legs after a particularly hard hill race. He offered me a simple remedy, "Try walking down backwards."

It was also not uncommon to hear about local athletes bathing their feet in the salt waters of Loch Linnhe, a tip inherited from Eddie on how to cure blistered feet.

Eddie was not only a great athlete, he was also a great organiser and this was recognised by the Lochaber Sports Council when they presented him with the Service to Sport award, an accolade that was richly deserved.

Eddie Campbell's life revolved around the two things he loved most, his family and his running. His legendary achievements on Ben Nevis are unlikely to be equalled. In 1995, when Eddie ran into Claggan Park to finish his 44th Ben Nevis Race the applause from the crowd was ten times greater than that of the winner.

Shortly after this year's Race, I saw Eddie strolling along the banks of the River Nevis. He did not see me and I did not interrupt his solitude; he looked at peace beneath the mountain he had climbed so many times, the mountain that had given him a lifetime of pleasure. Each time I climb to the summit, I will see through the mist Eddie's white beard and friendly smile, and I will hear his words "Keep the trot going, Graham."

Eddie Campbell was one of God's special people and he was special to all who knew him. Just as William Swan's name has been remembered for the last hundred years, so will Eddie Campbell's for the next hundred.

"When I think of The Ben I can visualise
Eddie descending in a pair of "gloshers",
it's been in my mind for years and will
remain for the rest of my life!"

Joss Naylor

There can be no better tribute to Eddie...

...than taking part in the Ben Nevis Race in his memory and Joss Naylor hopes to do just that in 2006 on his 70th birthday. Here is what Joss writes...

"Eddie Campbell was part of Ben Nevis, it was his life to run 44 Ben races and to complete them was great. I was talking to Jim Smith one day and he said he had run over forty Bens but would not take Eddie's record, which I thought was great respect for the man. Fort William is not the same place and without Eddie I feel out of place there. When I did the Three Peaks record in 1972, Eddie was there to see me off and wish me well. It was a dirty wet night, mist down to 500ft. I may run The Ben when I am 70 just to appreciate the lifetime of Eddie and the pleasure he gave to so many people. I would like to see a statue in Fort William to remember his obsessions – they were all for the right reasons. May this man's spirit live forever. It's when you write these type of things, it brings a tear to your eyes and makes you realise our souls are one."

Joss is pictured here with "Fly" and his support group on the "60 at 60" event. Bill Smith, Ben runner and author of "Stud Marks on the Summits", mentions that the reason that there was no profile of Eddie in his book is because Eddie was too modest to take part in spite of badgering. Eddie did write a book himself – Ben Nevis Races 1951-60. It starts poignantly by paying respects to those no longer here, but whose endeavour and assistance helped Ben Nevis running reach such "heights". Typically of Eddie, the race results have amusing asides like *"A distance of just over 10 miles (give or take a zigzag)"*. His comment for

this photo on the left of the 1953 start is *"The late Mr John (Jock) Petrie set the runners off with a double-barrel shotgun, which all the runners made sure he was pointing upwards"*. Number 5 (looking away!) is D. Dando who, Eddie said, was closer to him at the summit than his shadow. They finished 1st and 2nd, with Eddie 7mins ahead in 1hr 53mins 18secs.

Photo courtesy of Gillian Naylor

Graham's display for Eddie and the Ben Race in the Fort William Swimming Pool

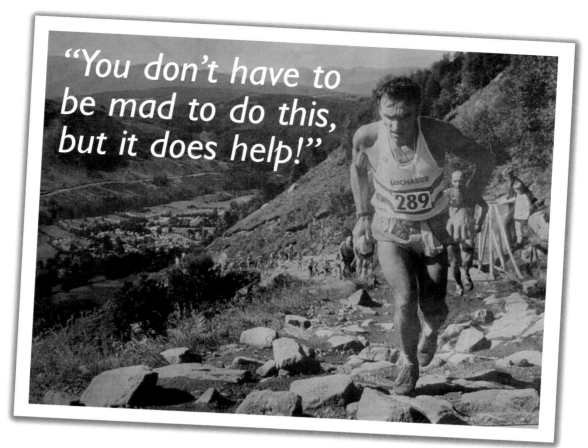

'96 photo of Graham (10th) courtesy of Peter Hartley (himself a top ten man, being 9th in '78).
Peter's photo of Andy Beaty at this same spot was displayed in the Millenium Dome – 2x1 metres!

This adorns the wall above Graham Brooks' desk at work and is a cutting taken from the Independent, previewing a new (June '04) book on fell running by Richard Askwith, the paper's Associate Editor. Straight away Graham (above) sent off for "Feet in the Clouds" and Richard states in the book how he enjoyed reading all the tales about Eddie. Richard describes right from the start when he was once caught in a vicious storm in a training run. He was saved by saying to himself "think of Eddie Campbell, trotting through Glencoe snowstorms in his plimsolls, with just a handful of boiled sweets in his anorak pocket to stave off hypothermia".

Richard mentions Eddie's adventures like... the terrible cramp Eddie suffered in a marathon, so he finished the race running backwards (John MacRae running after him with a saltcellar)! The time Eddie was offered a map saying it was as much use to him as the Oban Times! The fact that he always seemed to be running through deep snow without very many clothes. Calling his "no-way-would-you-ever-get-a-permit" races, training runs! His weather philosophy – "Let it pour!"

Richard ran in the 2003 Ben Nevis Race himself and got a red-hot tip on how to descend the mountain from Pete Bland – "Disengage brain!" He did a good time of 2hrs 15mins 24secs, 183rd place, and I laughed to read in his book he would have been 12th woman had he been one!

FEET IN THE CLOUDS
A TALE OF FELL-RUNNING AND OBSESSION

Eric Whitehead's photo on the cover of Richard's book has got folk guessing... is it Joss or Selwyn Wright? Selwyn says, "it should remain an anonymous runner on an anonymous fell. Isn't the reality that it represents all of us? Or am I just an old romantic?"

Over to you, Mr (and Mrs) Starter.
Ready, steady,

BANG!

Sir Donald Campbell, so very popular, died last year, 2004.

This is my favourite start picture (1973) as it reflects the spirit of The Ben – the camaraderie. Number 67 Harry Blenkinsop of Sale Harriers, 146 Nigel Chisholm of Lochaber, 63 Arthur Leyton of Vauxhall Motors and extreme right Jim Smith of Bury all went on to be Connochie Plaque holders for 21 Ben Nevis Races. Little did Nigel think, as he lined up looking at Colonel Cameron of Lochiel, that 30 years later in 2003 he would be sending us off himself! For health and safety reasons he was given a little horn instead of a pistol! Here is Nigel (right) in full splendour in Claggan Stores after the race! Nigel ran his first Ben Race in 1960 so almost featured in SIX decades of Ben running! Here are a few of the other Starters over the years:

Top row:
1994 Paul Sommerville, Commercil Director of ScotRail.
1977 HRH The Duke of Kent.
1979 Kenneth McKellar.
2001 Brian Kearney &
1953 Provost MacFarlane.
Middle row:
1988 Norris Beith, North British Hotels Trust.
Bottom row:
1953 Jock Petrie.
1972 Doctor Connochie.
2002 James Martin, aged 88 and pictured running in 1937.

Photo courtesy of the Press and Journal

No need for a left to right description here! The occasion is the tercentenary celebrations of Fort William being called Fort William! Sir Jimmy (silvery) Savile is looking a bit dimensionally challenged, but actually it was a cardboard cut-out he'd sent along as he couldn't attend in person! Eddie's widow Chrissie is pictured between Eddie and Her Majesty The Queen on a not so long ago day in 1990. Chrissie started us off in the Eddie Campbell Memorial Race in 1997 and presented the prizes afterwards to a great ovation.

Another lady Starter was "Madame Ecosse" herself, Winnie Ewing, (left) in 1984, with fellow politician Sir Russell Johnston (above right) having done the honours in 1978. The year after Winnie Ewing, the star attraction was Hercules the Bear!

Jumping away back to the early days, the races were set off with a shotgun! The date of this one on the right is 1903 and the place is Achintee where these seven contestants are about to be set off up The Ben by the shotgun wielded by Major Cameron, the Factor of the Cameron Lucy Estate. Imagine the fright of that gun going off behind! It would give me a good ten yard lead! But only for ten yards, because these are the top players. This race, to the summit only, was won by the gentleman on the left, Ewen Mackenzie, the Observatory road-man. Ewen went on later in the same year to set a record for the Ben from the Old Post Office and back in 2 hours 10 mins. That record was never beaten for 36 years! Scientists did tests on him and worked out that he developed one third of a horsepower!

Photo courtesy of the Royal Meterological society

The third runner from the right in the race photo on the previous page is a man who holds a great place of honour in the chronicles of The Ben Race – the man who started it all, William Swan. This is Willie pictured in later life outside his barber's shop and you can imagine what the talk would be about whilst you were under the razor – trusting he wouldn't get too carried away! His advertisement in the papers stated:

Walking-Sticks in Great Variety.
Ben Nevis Walking-Sticks Specially adapted for climbing.

————

N.B.—Full information given to Visitors intending to Climb the Ben by calling at the above Address.

The shop directly opposite Willie's in the High Street was MacFarlane the Chemist's and in their advert they boasted:

Sole Proprietor of the BEN NEVIS SPRING TABLE WATERS. Patronised by Royalty. Recommended by the Faculty. The best in the Kingdom.

So it **IS** true about the water!

Willie was the first man to try a timed run to the summit and back, recording 2 hours 41 mins, which is fantastic on an unbearably hot day at the end of September 1895. He had a Bovril at the top rather than a refreshment of his rival shopkeeper's wares!

Concluding our selection of starters from the 100+ years of Ben racing is the poor man who never got to pull the trigger! Here we all are on the right, lined up in front of Mr Kenneth Graham, the Managing Director of Whyte & MacKay Distillers Ltd. He was to have started the 1980 race but it was cancelled as this dramatic photo below shows:

At the halfway checkpoint, Donald Watt of the Lochaber Mountain Rescue seems to be relaying to the park "No way!" as John Hinde, who had been team leader of RAF Kinloss, directly behind Donald looks askance. He'll be wondering how his daughter Fiona and future son in law Roger Wild in the line up will take the news. John sadly died recently after coming back from the hills he so loved.

"How's about that then?"

Sir Jimmy Savile's catch phrase is true to life when he competed in the Half Way Ben race for many years. Sir Jimmy is Chieftain of the Lochaber Games held in July each year. He is warming up before the start of the race, recording the radio programme he had on Sundays in the '70s, Savile's Travels, so that is a microphone he is holding rather than the famous cigar. The cigar was to the fore even after a day's "yomping" with the Marines, where he'd be draped over the bonnet of his Rolls Royce lighting up! Sir Jimmy was an honorary "Sar'nt Major" of the Marines and had earned the respect of all with his manner and fitness. Sir Jimmy's memories of Eddie and The Ben are nicely summed up in his note — "fixing it" for "Up The Ben wi' Eddie"…

"Ben Nevis! Wow! Britain's highest mountain. The name means so much to so many different people. My first trip up the Ben, on a snowy February day, saw me accidentally marooned for twenty seven hours on my own. Not a good start for a love affair that's lasted over forty years.

The Great Glen of Lochaber, home of Ben Nevis has always been a place of magic for me. So much so that I now live on the other side of the hill in Glencoe.

The first twenty six years of me being the Chieftain of the Highland Games on a Saturday was followed by the Half Ben race on the Sunday. Far too tempting for me to miss. Being a rubbish hill runner, I finished last every single year. Who cares! I only saw Eddie at the start — he was too fast for me, but often would I use the beacon of his light hair to show me the way to go up the track. They altered the day of the race so I only had twenty six years of coming last.

What memories!"

Another TV star is Cal Macaninch (centre) who featured in the successful Mountain Rescue drama — Rockface. He presented the prizes for the 2002 Ben after running in it himself and finishing in the top half of the field which is more than can be said for me. I got him to autograph my certificate …

Stevie Macleod (left of photo) was a champion boxer bringing his determination to The Ben and often being well placed. Here he is (right), pleased as punch, coming in first local in 1985 in a great time of 1hr 37mins 35secs in 29th place.

The very first picture to be reproduced in the LAC journal — the Ed. suggested colouring it in, but not showing the results to Steve!

"Stout" heart in the Hielan's...

Photo courtesy of John MacRae

...belonging to Kenny Campbell (in kilt on right) as he made his ascent to the summit of The Ben with this beer barrel on the only day the Ben Race has ever been cancelled, 1980.

Since 1971, strongman Kenny from Sutherland had kept the press and the public amused by carrying various heavy things to the top in aid of Cancer Research.

Kenny, no relation to Eddie, is pictured above resting beyond the halfway and is photographed in action in the newspaper cutting. The barrel weighed 1½ cwt and was to have been a warm up for Kenny carrying it from Land's End to John o' Groats. I spoke to him at the top of The Ben and asked him if he was going ahead with his marathon End to End walk as it had said in the papers. **"NO WAY!"** he said. Kenny earlier had received letters from the council, when he had left his big organ on the summit years before, for him to remove it. There was no need for them to write this time with the beer as the Mountain Rescue volunteered!

An earlier effort to pull this piano up ended in near disaster... Kenny had made a kind of guider arrangement with bicycle wheels and had put the rope to pull it with round his neck. You've already guessed what was going to happen! The piano took off over the edge of the track and dragged Kenny after it, just stopping feet away from a 400 foot drop!

So it was back to the drawing board, and this time Kenny set off carrying a 200 pound organ (I don't know if that is lbs or £s)...

86

The determination was just as great and the kilt just as short...

...when Kenny set out again in August 1971, a month after his previous piano concert! Days of epic struggle later, Kenny sat at his organ, bruised and battered, playing loudly and proudly "Scotland the Brave" on the summit. He said that encouragement from people on the mountain, and the knowledge that Cancer Research was such a good cause, kept him going. Now comes the bit I referred to earlier in the beer barrel story... Kenny finished his tune and closed the lid and, like Elvis, "left the building". Letters, at first heated, went back and fore about removing the organ, but then a sense of fun crept in and the council said they would sponsor Big Kenny to go up and deliver the organ to the dump. Up went Kenny only to find all that was left were two little planks of wood – the rest had been taken by souvenir hunters!

Apart from organs, wheelbarrows, cars etc. etc. being heaved, lifted and driven up, The Ben is subject to all kinds of things. Celebration bonfires have never really been lucky with the weather – for Queen Victoria's Diamond Jubilee in 1897, soldiers went up in full regalia to find 2 feet of snow and this was 22nd of June! Pre-digital days, the plate camera could not battle against the driving sleet in the fierce south-westerly, so the occasion was never recorded. At last came the order to stand down and the troops bundled into the Summit Hotel! The bonfire, which should have been visible from Ireland, could only just be seen as a dull glow from the hotel window! For Edward VII's Coronation on 9th August 1902, fireworks were set off as well as the bonfire – *"Futile!"* said Wm. Kilgour, looking out of the Observatory window as the rain lashed the bedraggled party of "Toon Cooncillors" and Freemasons. For Queen Elizabeth's Coronation in 1953, John Macdonald can remember getting a day off school to assist in carrying 200 fifteen-foot long trees up The Ben! Not only that, but also a quarter of a ton of radio equipment, so that the event could be broadcast to the world! And when the 2nd of June came, guess what, *"the bonfire was visible only to those on the summit!"* These are the words of the late George MacPherson (left), whom Lady Ben Racer Kathleen Connochie married. Kate said that they first met when she "literally bumped into him" as she went through the door for the "after the race dance" in 1955 at the Town Hall – itself the scene of a fine blaze when it got burnt to the ground! The earliest bonfire recorded on The Ben was in 1842 for Queen Victoria's first grand tour of Scotland. As well as all the wood, tar barrels were taken up (this is long before the Pony Track) and it is described in a Memorial descriptive as *"...and ever and anon, as the breeze cleared them (passing clouds) away, it burst forth with Vesuvian splendour, and shed a red glare on every mountain top around."* Hip, hip, Hooray!

George at his happiest – marking Ben races! The late Ian Donald is the runner.

Juan & Ricard...

...are also carrying a musical instrument up – but not as vast or as heavy as Kenny's! They come from the Costa Del Sol so would feel at home with this lovely day in July. I asked them what they were going to play on their guitar at the top and they chorused **"FREEDOM!"**

Allan MacRae (pic 1.) has good reason to join in with the cries of "freedom", as he was the leading light in the crofters of Lochinver, his home, having a buy-out of the Assynt Estate in 1992.

Allan is pictured again (pic 2.) on the right of Ronald (Cammy) Campbell after coming 12th to Cammy's 10th in the 1974 Ben Nevis Race. The toast was in orange juice rather than "the water of life" as in the photo of Allan + dog – that would come later at Eddie's famous post-race party! At one of the parties, a nurse discovered a runner had a gap in his leg - it was broken, so he got taken to the Belford!

Allan won the Ben Race in 1966 and for training used to get up very early in the morning before work on the Hydro-Electric dams and run up a handy hill! He was no lover of road sections and said in his highland voice after the Mamore Race, which finishes with 7 miles on the road down the side of Loch Leven - "I wass all right until I hit the road!" That didn't deter him from going down to the fairly flat 18 mile "Three Towers Race" starting at Horwich in Lancashire. The only snag he found there was the amount of petrol his huge Jaguar went through! As that race was held in October, Eddie also went down and used to fill his minibus with customers for a holiday to see the Blackpool Illuminations, making a wee detour to take in the race!

It was Allan and Eddie that would decide who would run for the Lochaber A team – at stake in 1969 for the first time were gold medals. Their dilemma was the lad on the right... Donald A. Fraser. The previous year, Donald had been a wonderful 6th place, causing the winner, Mike Davies, to remark, "Donald is a potential winner and has everything it takes – skill, stamina and determination," but the problem in 1969 was that he also had chicken pox! Running to halfway the Saturday before the race, Donald literally crawled on his hands and knees across the Red Burn. Eddie coming behind him said *"Give up or you're going to kill yourself."*

By the next Saturday, Donald had rested and Allan called him to one side and said *"we haff picked the four for the team."*

"Oh yes." said Donald. *"Yes,"* said Allan, *"myself, Eddie and John Marstrand along with yourself."* *"But what if I fizzle out?"* Donald questioned. *"We know you, Tonald, and we don't want beaten by our own B team!"*

They won! Donald (pic 3.) receives a gift from Chrissie Campbell going to South Africa.

1.

2.

3.

No cries of "**Freedom!**" for Quinny

Photo courtesy of Ian Quinn

When Ian was five years old, his father was one of "The Seven Men of Knoydart" who took possession of farm land which had been requisitioned by the Government during the war and was about to be turned back over to an unpopular landowner. The seven men each staked out 15 acres but had to withdraw when they were served with "interim interdicts" from the Court of Session. Here is Ian (right) when he ran the Ben Race in 1964. He did well – being 38th in 2hrs 5mins 15secs. Ian rested on his laurels at that and didn't compete again. He had discovered CARS! Cars have been his whole life and he is the popular proprietor of "Lochaber School of Motoring". His photo, his certificate, his programme and his results sheet are high among his souvenirs – all a part of The Ben's mighty rich tapestry. Ian in the photo is heading off for a shower and a hot cup of tea to warm up after a wet day! The Ben Race is sponsored by Brooke Bond Scottish Blend Tea, but if you are offering a cuppa to another local runner, John Hepburn (below right), one thing you must never do is to ask "One lump or two?" in case he thinks you're refering to his ankle. Poor John had been setting great store by his build up for the 2003 Ben Race – doing several very good times in training on The Ben and finishing high up in National Championship races and getting a fab 43rd place in the World Veteran Hill Running Championships after cycling to the start – in Germany!

Closer to home, disaster struck him just before Ben Nevis Race day when he twisted his ankle. He was running along the river bank and finished up with a lump on his ankle the size of a balloon! As you see in the photo of the "Y2K" race, John is running strongly down to Achintee from the stile, holding off Horwich runner, Steve Jackson to finish 8th in 1hr 40mins – the pair of them have had great ding-dongs in and around the top ten for years. So in 2003 when John couldn't compete because of his twisted ankle, Steve didn't have his sparring partner to lift him to greater things, finishing outside the top ten medals in 11th place, behind consistent local runner, shepherd Peter Kennedy. Steve is a proud recipient of the Connochie Plaque, having done his 21st Ben in 1999.

Photo courtesy of John Hepburn

Pacemaker extraordinaire,...

...that is Roger Boswell! In the photo, taken by Mark Rigby, who is himself a "roundsman", you can see Roger and Adrian Belton approaching halfway down The Ben. Adrian was on his way to completing a round of 28 Munros in under 24 hours! Adrian, in the patriotic pants, didn't appreciate the leg tangling properties of Toby and Banjo, Roger's dogs! These rounds all started when Philip Tranter, son of the Scottish historical novelist Nigel Tranter, set a target for people to follow of doing The Ben plus all the hills in the Aonach, Mamore and Grey Corries groups in under 24 hours. Other runners extended Tranter's Round (as if it wasn't enough!) to include further away Munros, the hills above 3000ft. Ramsay's Round now became the challenge – Charlie Ramsay had a celebratory get-together in July 2003 for the 25th anniversary of doing his round. Without fail all the runners throughtout Britain who seek to increase the number of hills will enlist the help of the Welsh Wizard – that's our Roger. Roger Boswell moved to Fort William from Wales in 1977 and heard about the Ben Nevis Race but had never been up. It was now the Thursday before the race and up went Roger to run to the top. When he was at halfway he spied another runner away below him. Next thing Roger was astonished when the runner was soon overhauling him. It was Mike Short of Horwich RMI and Mike waited for Roger at the top. They then jogged down together chatting, with Roger getting tips from the great fell runner who never quite won The Ben. Mike was 2nd that year – his 3rd in a row of 4 second places as he was the same again in '78. Roger came 11th in his 1st Ben and was 1st local, being 1st local again the following year in an improved position of 5th. Eddie's first training run on The Ben is remarkably similar to Roger's as he too saw a little figure away below in the distance. Next thing , just like for Roger, the runner came up alongside Eddie and his two guides, Charlie and Allan Petrie. The runner who caught them up was none other than Duncan MacIntyre. They had started at 5.30 on the Sunday morning (!) and Duncan reckoned that the rocks were too frosted to go higher (this being April 1951) and advised everyone to turn and go down. Which they did, Eddie saying *"Not so much admitting defeat as doing what I was told!"*

I gave myself similar advice to curb my excitement when there was a stationary cloud over the summit of The Ben for a few days in May...

Wed 14th May '03 *Similar conditions to last two days with the stationary cloud at second zigzag making it the third trip into your own personal winter wonderland. Folk down below in the Fort are having their normal sunshine and showers, unaware of what it's like up here. It is exciting to come back into it again! From the third zigzag the snow was deep enough to cover the rocks which guide you where the path is and the cold wind and snow were filling up the footprints of other walkers on the route. It left only a little track about a foot wide of small indentations in the snow and to lose that would have you wandering in the near white out if no map and compass.*

*If the track is disappearing, go back and return another day – **The Ben will still be there!***

The Emperor Napoleon said much the same thing as he retreated from Moscow – "That's the last time I ever go anywhere out of season!"

"Goggles" the dog

I shared a Mars bar with Goggles (wearing snow glasses) one day in May. She was a fine asset up there for finding the path in such conditions. How much easier it would be if we humans could just bend down and sniff instead of getting out the map and compass!

REMEMBER.. OUT OF SEASON YOU MUST HAVE THE KNOWLEDGE !

The Observatory

Gardyloo Gully

Tower Gully

Pony Track

2000ft STRAIGHT DOWN

You see the danger in that you can't go in a straight line from **A** to **B** at the top! Be warned, because there are conditions where you can see the Observatory buildings in front of you but you do not see the gullies with their snow cornices in between!

Photo courtesy of Alex Gillespie

91

Helena, Bodie and Rudie...

...are into magical mystical mountains! They are from California. I spent a great time with them swopping myths and legends. They were making their way up late in the day - deliberately so they could meet any fairies who might come out! Rudie, standing the highest, has imagined himself firstly at the halfway "lake" then on the top. He had gone up in a flight of fancy. The rest of the family chipped in *"delusional!"*

However for us that cannot Astral-project, we must knuckle down to the job in hand like these walkers approaching "Black Rock," which was a timing point in the old days of Ben racing. One time I went up with my "I am Spock" tee-shirt on, I could have made a mint from the requests of people for me to beam them up!

As to myths and legends,...

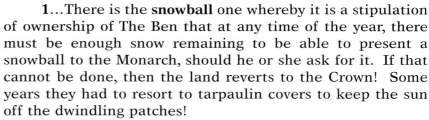

...only a few apply directly to The Ben.

1...There is the **snowball** one whereby it is a stipulation of ownership of The Ben that at any time of the year, there must be enough snow remaining to be able to present a snowball to the Monarch, should he or she ask for it. If that cannot be done, then the land reverts to the Crown! Some years they had to resort to tarpaulin covers to keep the sun off the dwindling patches!

2...In some of the hidden corries, snow will remain all year round because the sun never shines into them. When you hear the expression "deer haunts", it conjures up an image of just such a place – the sort of gully high on The flanks of The Ben that was home to the **"Hag of the Speckled Mountain"**! She lived off milk from the hinds and meeting her on a misty day wasn't necessarily all bad, as she could grant you good luck as well as ill.

3...A sure way to have good luck is to find **"lucky white heather"** and if you keep your eyes peeled as you go up you may spot some. White heather came about from a sad long ago tale of lost love, when the lovely Malvina was told that her fiancé Oscar had died in battle. She ran and ran over the hills and every time a tear fell, so the heather turned from purple to white. Malvina made a wish, "May this white heather forever bring good fortune to all those who find it."

4...The halfway loch has strange **hoof marks** in the rocks and some believe they were made by the Kelpies – water horses. They would appear to weary travellers and nuzzle away at folks' arms until the people were tempted to ride them – straight into deep water never to be seen again!

5...It's no myth that children don't like Brussels sprouts, but mothers in Fort William of old had the perfect answer... From the foot of the north face cliffs, the Allt a' Mhuilinn runs past the halfway loch and down to the sea. It used to be called a different Gaelic name meaning **"Donald of the Sugar"**. The mention of this name would terrify the youngsters and they would do anything rather than face the threat of *"Donald of the Sugar will come and get you!"* Modern day mums simply mention the name of the town's driving examiner and the kids all gobble up their greens!

6...There is one myth I can dispel right away – of the Ben Nevis runner who is kept locked up in a cage and only let out on race day. **Cammy** is not that bad! But if one were to arrive at a stile the same time as him, I'd advise "after you" to avoid the legendary elbows! The opposite occurred in a clash between two of the great Ben Race masters – Mike Davies and Peter Hall, with seven victories on The Ben between them in the '60s. Peter was leading Mike in the Yorkshire 3 Peaks Race and had held a gate open for Mike. What sportsmanship – or was it gamesmanship? Here is the story of Cammy's first Ben race and it is indeed a study in determination...

"We talked of Cannon

Norman

Finalyson

and Walker"

It was September 1970 at the old King George V Park that myself and Neil MacDonald (Conger, as he was known to everyone) watched the runners finishing the race, we both decided to have a go.

Our training over the winter prior to the 1971 race consisted of nightly road runs and a cross-country league race on Sundays organised by Lochaber A.C. These races started from the old King George V pavillion and consisted of different races round the Peat Track either way and up Glen Nevis, all in all they were very enjoyable and were fiercely competitive.

January 1971 arrived and I was much involved with my other sport of shinty. I played nearly every Saturday so thus did not compete in any races. My training was consisting of 5-8 mile road runs at night with circuit training on Tuesday nights. As the brighter nights arrived myself and Neil would take the bus into Claggan and change at the Repeater Station, then run to Half-Way and back, most times racing each other. Neil had a bit of a disadvantage as he was a twenty cigarettes a day man, however he enjoyed his running whatever position he finished.

The Half Ben race was approaching shortly so we trained quite regularly on The Ben itself, come hail or rain we were both dedicated in our aim to run the full Ben. Some days after a really hard day's work (N.B: Cammy started his own slater's business after coming out of the RAF) I didn't feel like training but Neil would always coax me out and I was glad he did. Our excitement was building up as we talked of Cannon, Norman, Finlayson and Walker, all the top fell runners at this time.

The day of the Half Ben arrived. The weather was very dull, but dry conditions looked good for us, we would get a good indication of how our training was going. There was a big entry and the favourite was Dave Cannon of Kendal who was second to Jeff Norman in the previous year's Ben Nevis Race. Sure enough, Cannon led from start to finish, but not before Brian Finlayson had given him a good fight. I myself was delighted to finish 5th, just behind Allan MacRae a previous winner of the Ben.

I knew I was reasonably fit but I knew that the full Ben would be a different and harder race, the one good thing was that the race would start for the first time from the New Town Park, thus cutting out a fair bit of distance on the road.

I continued to train and would run to the top of The Ben every night, I had consistent training times of 1hr 45mins to 1hr 47mins. Thinking those were great times I let Eddie know what I was doing but alas he reckoned going to the top every night was not on and also I had to get one good time of around 1hr 40mins at least once a week and never mind the other times. As normal I didn't listen and continued to train as I thought fit, my excitement getting greater in anticipation of the big day as it grew nearer.

In August I ran at the Police Sports at Claggan, all the competitors were Lochaber A.C. members. The race was a fairly even pace until the last lap when Eugene McEvoy made a break and I had to summon a sprint finish on the home straight to win. The following Saturday I competed in the 1500m and 800m at the Nairn Games and gained two victories.

I was now looking forward to the Big Race, runners started to come up to train a few days before the race, the posters advertising the race were everywhere. All the locals were offering "All the best Cammy", my neighbours and friends were all going to watch the race. I began to worry maybe I'd have a terrible run and let everyone down.

On the Friday night before the race I collected the Race Programme, and there it was "R. Campbell, Lochaber A.C.". I was now really on a knife edge, but I thought, have an early night and you'll be fine in the morning.

Saturday morning, Race day had finally arrived. I looked out of my *bedroom window, it's a good day and The Ben stands majestically straight in front, and it's clear on the top. I got up about 9.30 had my cornflakes and toast and now the adrenalin was flowing. I decided to just lounge around all morning and save all my energy for the Race. I must have looked through the programme a hundred times, I just didn't know how well I was going to run. I decided I would just run as hard as I could and hope for the best. One o'clock and I packed all my kit and double checked I'd got everything. My next door neighbour came in and wished me the best of luck and gave me a little horse-shoe for luck.*

At the field there was a big crowd assembled, I got changed and warmed up by myself. I didn't really want to talk to anyone before the start. After the checking of numbers we were finally on the start line ready to go. I had made sure I was on the front row so I could get a good start.

On your marks – Bang! – we were off. I went away fairly fast, lying about 8th going round the field. I could hear shouts of encouragement for me, it made me feel good. I could see Dave Cannon leading already, he looked so easy and effortless, I felt as if I was still sprinting.

Onto the road, along to Achintee I'm lying about 10th but I'm puffing and blowing a fair bit and we haven't reached the bottom of the hill yet. Illusions come flashing through my mind that everyone will pass me as soon as we start climbing. As we reach the car park I'm feeling really terrible, shouts of encouragement don't make me feel any better.

As we start to climb past the farm I am really struggling, four or five runners pass me, they seem fresh and full of running, still I decide to get my head down and get stuck in, in the hope I'll run out of my bad patch. After what seemed an eternity I reached the first short-cut above the hostel, my condition hadn't changed but at least nobody else had passed me and I'm lying about 13th, as we approach the broken bridge I hear a familiar voice behind, it's Charlie Jarvie, as he passes he gives a few grunts and signals me to stick in behind him, which makes me put in a little bit more effort. Around the shoulder and I'm still hanging on to Charlie for all my worth, my lungs feel they are going to burst, there's no relenting. I'm running and walking up to the burn, hell, I feel like packing in just now. Any thoughts of that begin to go as I look ahead and see other runners on their hands and knees, maybe they're just as knackered as me, anyhow they're not that far ahead, maybe I'll get some of them on the descent. If I can keep this position I know I'll come down fast, anyhow the main thing at the moment is to concentrate on getting to the summit. I think to myself that if I can stick with Charlie to the summit I'll be in a challenging position for the top ten.

As we pass half way I'm still fighting hard, but every part of my body is sore, I never realised the race was so hard, but although I'm feeling knackered no-one else has passed me for ages. The mountain rescue boys shout to us we're going well, if only they knew!

Onto the plateau now and I begin to realise that I'm going to reach the summit. I'm surprised there's so many people about just watching the race, still – it's really fine and clear on the summit, and some are having a picnic, others are busy with their cameras.

I reckon another four or five minutes and I'll reach the summit, just then I see Dave Cannon coming hammering down, he seems so fresh, he's well clear, myself and Charlie are now moving quite well and all my pain seems to be forgotten now as I see a large crowd on the summit. About four hundred yards from the checkpoint, I hear a shout of encouragement from a well known voice, that of Willie Anderson, this makes me put in a little sprint and I briefly pass Charlie who is now also putting in an extra effort.

As I come up to the checkpoint I feel good as the crowd clap and cheer, I grab my tag, slip it over my neck and then start to chase after Charlie who has now gained about 10 yards on me, someone shouts "fourteenth" so now it's all on for a good descent. I'm feeling not bad now, I can see other runners just ahead of us, I sense we'll catch them shortly.

A lot of other runners still going up shout that we're not far behind. Eddie shouts to get cracking, so we're both flying down now and quickly pass two runners, just then over to the left of me I see someone really tanking down, boulders flying everywhere. He looks a fairly old bloke, hell, we can't be going that well as he leaves us in his wake, however we soon pass another before half-way, we're lying 11th and 12th now and I can see a few runners ahead at the top of the grassy slope.

We pass another half way down the slope and then another at the bottom who is lying on his back really exhausted, a quick glance tells me it's Ian MacMillan of Invicta. My excitement is now mounting as I now have a real chance of making the top ten.

Over the broken bridge and Charlie still leads me but I'm feeling strong and I decide to pass him. "Keep it going" he manages to shout out, he's

Cammy
"so now it's all on for a good descent"

Photo courtesy of The Fell Runner

beginning to die also. I keep pushing hard and I quickly pass someone I recognise as Harry Walker, this gives me a great boost and I really hammer down the short cut and onto the path. I know I'm in eigth place and I'm closing on the seventh man who I recognise as Russell of Aberdeen University. He's about fifty yards ahead but he's coming back fast as we reach Achintee Farm. There's a large crowd cheering and shouting, it's a great feeling, but now as I hit the hard road my legs are feeling really drained, I'm down to a *jog and my legs feel like lead, the runners ahead are now going away from me, but I don't care, as all I want to do now is just finish and sit down.*

As I reach the small hill at the end of the straight I am reduced to a walk. I begin to panic a bit but I manage to get jogging again, but I'm really out on my feet now, I see the crowd at the Repeater Station and I hear the locals shouting and urging me on. I struggle on, praying no-one will pass me now. At last I reach the Repeater Station and what a welcome sight I see, the park is crowded with people and I hear the pipe band playing, into the field now and what a great feeling, someone shouts they're closing fast, I try to go faster but alas I'm completely drained. About thirty yards to the finish now and the crowd is shouting me on as I sense someone's catching me fast. There's nothing I can do, Harry Walker and Norman Carrington go steaming past me, I'm disappointed I've lost two places but I'm relieved at finally finishing.

I collapse after I finish and lie on the grass for about ten minutes and say to myself that's the last time I run this race. As I slowly recover and watch the other runners finishing I begin to feel proud at finishing 10th at my first attempt.

Allan MacLean comes up and tells me I've won the Newcomer Award, this makes me feel great and all these aches and pains and the bad memories are gone for the moment. I then learn that Lochaber have won the team award also and I am the third counter with Brian Finlayson and Allan MacRae.

The one thing I do know now is that the Ben Nevis Race is tough – bloody tough!

In these pages you have accompanied Cammy up The Ben and notice how he sought Eddie out for advice (even 'though he didn't take it!). Now Cammy in his turn dispenses his "sporting snippets" to others – Billy and Davy Rodgers, John Brooks, Steven Burns and many other great runners are all "Cammy's men". If you are wondering how Charlie Jarvie got on after his pell-mell descent with Cammy – he finished next in 11th place. The man lying exhausted in the Red Burn, Ian MacMillan, got himself up and out and came in 12th. Eddie was 48th and Cammy's training pal "Conger" was 60th, just in front of me - my excuse was picking up Conger's fag ends!

Notice on the photos of Dave Cannon and Harry Walker that they have the yellow strings round their necks... Cammy had said in his story "I grabbed my tag" and that is what used to happen. The marshals standing at the top dispensed the strings as the runners arrived, until one year there was a big panic when the bundle of tags all got knotted up and the runners were coming! So it was changed to the runners going up with a tag with their number on it and handing it over at the top. To be bang up to date runners now get "chipped" with an electronic tag clamped onto your wrist to plonk into a computer at the top and at the finish. A little strip of paper appears straight away with all your particulars on it – summit time and finish time. At the prize giving we laughed when they said that all you ones that have been tagged have to be in bed by 9 o'clock!

Photo on right painlessly removing old style tag!

The *Field* of Cairns

No 317 has a splitting headache!
Photo courtesy of Alex Gillespie - joke by John MacRae!

A stroll up Ben Nevis by Graham Brooks

Above: *The Brooks Dynasty, John, Billy, Billy Snr, Graham and (inset) Kevin. All of them were under 2 hours in the 1997 Eddie Campbell Memorial Race – notice Kevin's T-shirt, "A farewell to Eddie". Photo courtesy of Graham's collection.*

Everyone remembers their first time at anything and here is Graham's description of his first Ben Nevis Race – be prepared to split your sides with laughter!

It was the first Saturday in September. I was standing amongst a crowd of three hundred and fifty bodies and the smell of garlic and liniment was overpowering. The assortment of brightly coloured shorts and vests were bobbing about impatiently; it was the start of the Ben Nevis Race. My last race had been a cross-country affair when I was a schoolboy. Now at the age of thirty, although nervous, I was confident that I could run the Ben.

As the starter's gun cracked, the runners sped out of the park and along the road to Achintee. This was where I made my first mistake. As I stopped to tie a shoelace, two dozen feet trampled me to the ground. I managed to roll into the sanctuary of the ditch. Having regained my composure I followed on behind a man with a long white beard, affectionally known as "Old Eddie". By the time I reached the mountain the pace had slowed dramatically, my nerves had gone but so had my lungs and legs. A lady with a pigtail trotted past. I felt a deep sense of shame. Then came a gent in his late fifties, remarking as he went, "you're doing well, lad!" My confidence was disappearing fast. I trudged wearily upwards amongst a long line of gasping breathless bodies. The leaders had long since disappeared.

As we climbed up the steep scree-slope a thick mist descended. A runner called over apprehensively, "which way?" "Follow the man in front," I

"A lady with a pigtail trotted past."

Photo courtesy of Alex Gillespie

replied. "But which man does the leader follow?" he answered. I had no more breath to deal with silly questions as I concentrated on climbing upwards. An ashen-faced runner spoke to me in a weak voice, "Have we much further to go?" "Not long now," I lied. I had no idea where the summit was, never mind how far. But the poor wretch looked as if he needed some encouragement.

Suddenly a runner appeared, hurtling downwards. The leaders had turned and were on their way back. I did not know which way to dive, right or left, as runners descended straight at me out of the mist. A few minutes later we emerged onto the plateau, a blue sky above. With my fears gone, new strength came into my legs and I broke into a trot. As I passed Gardyloo Gully I heard a shout of encouragement. I looked across and saw the face of Willie Anderson perched at the edge of a sheer thousand foot drop. I remember thinking that no sober man would possibly stand there like that. Willie was to stand there for the next ten Ben Nevis Races. As I approached the summit cairn I put on a false smile and remarked to the marshals as casually as humanly possible, "Grand day for a stroll, lads."

I then turned and ran back down the mountain. As I descended the rough scree, runners were staggering about in all directions, and the noise of falling rocks above spurred me on even faster. Then came the dreaded grassy slope, 800 feet of horrendous thigh pain or a green backside. I chose the latter.

At the bottom, a quick drink from the Red Burn and back onto the bridle path. As I neared the end of the mountain I felt a great sense of joy until I reached the road at Achintee. My legs turned to jelly and buckled. A passing runner shouted, "Keep going, only a mile left!" "Only a mile," I thought. Why did he have to remind me? I have heard it takes an average man ten minutes to walk a mile. It took me eleven to run that one. As I staggered round the park to the cheers of the crowd I heard a shout,

"Private or National Health, pal?"

Photo courtesy of Anthony Macmillan

"Watch your back!" A runner was attempting to outsprint me in the last fifty yards. As he drew alongside I looked at his foaming mouth and haggard, pained features and hoped to God I did not look like that.

As I lay flat on my back after crossing the finishing line someone shouted across, "How did you enjoy that run?" I closed my eyes and decided that the man was insane.

Pictures are of Ros Evans on her way to being 1st lady in 1982 (I was just out of shot behind her!) and Chief MO, Dr MacAskill, looking at Mike Nicholson from Kendal.

How many methods of descending The Ben can you spot?

"All the threes" Ernie Orr of Lochaber AC, declining the offer of a dram and a stretcher ride from Kenny and Anne-Elaine Gillespie, as he heads down after turning at the top.

The Chopper was taking off a poor runner who'd hurt an ankle.

In the days of the Observatory, Wm. T. Kilgour said disparagingly of the race "Is the game worth the candle?" But is he one to talk? Just look at the photo below from his book "Twenty Years on Ben Nevis" and understand that one observer actually applied a sail to his taboggan, nearly following when it took off over the edge! In fact the observers took a great interest in the race and all the other things that went on.

Another photo from Wm T's book shows more peaceful pursuits. This impromptu pingpong table was hewn from the snow on the roof of the Observatory!

Photo courtesy of Kenny Matheson

Photos courtesy of Royal Meteorological Society

Wouldn't this have been handy for the Observers nipping down to Fort William for a take-away!

Coming...

Photo courtesy of Dave McLaggan

Ex-Golden Lion army parachute team member Dave McLagan (on the left in the chopper) and friend Jim McConnell set a record for Britain's highest landing when they touched down on the summit of The Ben on 7th December 1987. Leaving the helicopter at 7,000 feet they had to ensure the wind was less than 12 knots – a tall order in December, but they needed a snow cover to protect them from "skinnt knees and jeellied nebs" on the rocky top! Jim's comment to the BBC cameras was amusing – *"Our preparations took four weeks for this and I will need another four to come back down to earth!"*

The pair raised money for the Post Viral Fatigue Syndrome Research Fund - their sponsor John Ritchie of Simpson Motors in Brechin was a sufferer and had launched the Tayside Coxsackie Support Group.

...and going

Photo courtesy of Davie Gardner

As a little aside to the story, AA patrolman Gordon Clark had something to tell his wife that night...

Gordon had been patrolling up Glen Nevis when a man appeared at the side of the road waving him to stop. "I can't get my engine started."

Ascertaining that the man was in the AA, Gordon told him to hop in and direct him to the beleaguered vehicle, to be told it was up a track "that way" his customer had said pointing in the direction of The Ben! Round a corner Gordon saw **the helicopter** and chuckled away to himself as he fixed on the jump leads. The engine roared into life and Gordon was given a tour around The Ben for his good deed.

"Not bad for an RAF pilot without a cockpit or parachute!"

Photo courtesy of Davie Gardner

These were the brave words of Squadron Leader Dave Willis (nearest us with the green sail) as the pair launched themselves off The Ben by running towards the edge of the cliff. Climber Davie Gardner from Milngavie in Glasgow was up there with his camera and recorded the moment, while down below on the Carn Dearg Arête, climber and photographer Alan Thomson from Ballachulish describes hearing "an eerie flutter" and fearing an avalanche looked up to see "the Icarus twins"! Alan spoke to the fliers later and learnt about the sport that from that day in February 1974 was to emerge as a new exciting challenge. A present day Fort William hang glider takes his dog with him and when he launches off, the dog zooms down the mountainside to meet him at the bottom!

Flying with Dave Willis was Gerry Breen, a junior technician in the RAF who kept his senior officer right and who went on to design his own hang gliders and to do "derring deeds" like flying off the Angel Falls in Venezuela and to fly micro-lights across the Iceland icecap.

The cold air of The Ben that day meant that they couldn't get the thermal uplift needed, so they landed at Polldubh in Glen Nevis instead of Claggan Park as planned. The 4½ mile flight, or "free abseil" as Alan describes it, lasted 8½ minutes and I listened avidly to a recording that Alex Gillespie (up The Ben following an overnight rescue) was given by Dave Willis, which Dave had made as he descended...

"Wonder if Gerry can hear me? GERRY! No."

Shrieks of "Mew mew" could be heard... "Just an eagle come to look at me!"

All this was delivered in a perfectly calm voice.

Alan asked about the big packs they were wearing and was told that they had 650 "first day covers" stamped envelopes to commemorate their record breaking flight, hoping to raise £1,000 for the RAF museum.

Pack of '82

The challenge went out to cubs and scouts the length and breadth of Britain to find the most unusual place to make tea. What better place for the Kilmallie cubs to come up with than the summit of The Ben? Not many other places have snow in summer to melt for that tasty brew!

Just who would act as guide for Senga's intrepid gang? The answer is a list of very well-known "Ben Nevis" names drawn from the boys' fathers...

Neil Gillespie on the extreme left and Liam Bruce on right of flag, with Iain Smith behind Senga.

Photo courtesy of Jimmy Smith

Neil
Truck
Driver

Liam
RAF

Iain
RAF

Photo courtesy of George Bruce

Photo courtesy of Cubby Images

A very apt leader that day would have been Dave "Cubby" Cuthbertson to take up the cubs and he is pictured on the left stunt doubling for both movie stars and starlets – look out for the blue dress next time this film comes on the telly! Cubby is also behind the cameras to make the films, often suspended in mid air! Ken Crocket describes Cubby in his book "Ben Nevis" as living *"for and by mountaineering"*.

Cubby tied a different knot on The Ben when he got married on the mountain. It should have been one of those idyllic days with the shrill song of the snow bunting welcoming the bridal party onto the summit – but alas it was the opposite. Plan B was put into operation when it was realised that all the guests wouldn't be able to get to the top. So now the guests were taken to the summit of Melantee, a couple of thousand feet lower. All that remained was to try to tell the bride and groom on Tower Ridge! Bride Jo tells the story...

105

We are all invited to the wedding of...

Dave (Cubby) Cuthbertson

Joanna George

Photo courtesy of Alex Gillespie

Here is how Jo describes her fantastic day...

"A few details about the wedding day! We got married on Ben Nevis on the 13th May 1995. Dave and I stayed in the CIC Hut the night before and a friend joined us. During the night it snowed heavily and by the morning The Ben was back in winter condition again! We were a little worried as we were climbing Tower Ridge and had planned to meet the wedding party at 11am! The climb was a lot of fun – my first time, but the weather steadily deteriorated. The plan was to get married on the summit. Some friends had taken various routes up the mountain to join us – some by climbs, others by the tourist path and those who didn't fancy the long hike, or were unable (we had some 80+ year olds and the youngest was only a few months!), were taken up by helicopter. A friend who worked for PLM, Dave Clem was fantastic – not only had offered us this service completely free of charge but on the return journey he even gave people a quick tour of the North Face. Anyhow eventually the weather got so bad that it was obvious the ceremony couldn't take place on the summit. Our best man, Paul Moores, together with Davie Clem, the pilot, tried to find us on the ridge to let us know the ceremony would have to be elsewhere. It was surreal for out of the mist appeared the helicopter. Davie touched down with one skid on the ridge and Paul leapt out, his kilt blowing up in the updraught – of course he was a true Scot! He broke the news, leapt back into the helicopter and off they went! We made it to the summit on time but then had to make our way to the new location Melantee.

I was whisked off and met by my father who walked me into the wedding party. It was amazing, the weather improved and the backdrop was impressive. Donald Macauley piped and in this setting the sound (and sight) was so impressive. The ceremony was very moving – I think more so because of our location.

Afterwards we made our way for lunch to The Factors House – some on foot... of course we flew this time!

While we were all sat round the table we noticed that one member was missing - my brother in-law's father! Thankfully Davie flew back and found him still walking down the tourist path – he was the oldest member of the wedding party – not a bad effort!

The day finished with a fantastic ceilidh at Glenfinnan House Hotel. Our wedding cake was us climbing Ben Nevis – it was a shame we had to cut into that fantastic mountain!

Really the whole idea of the wedding was to show our friends and family the mountain that we loved and to be married in the surroundings that brought us together."

What a day to remember! Jo adds that Dave is from Edinburgh but lived up in the area in the '80s which is how she met him. Joanna is from Salen (Ardnamurchan). When Jo met Dave she started climbing and together they toured around Scotland and Europe climbing and to this day climbing is still very much their lives. Jo was 26 when they married and Dave was 37.

Photos courtesy of Jo and Dave

> *"To some there is only till the following Saturday to race again – to others there is a full year!"*

That sounds like someone really obsessed with The Ben, but actually it was only me. It is always a proud moment to line up with the rest, but none more so than for Eddie's Memorial Race in 1997. On behalf of Lochaber Athletic Club, Leen Volwerk paid a wonderful tribute to Eddie in the programme:

A Tribute to Eddie Campbell
By Leen Volwerk

Eddie will not be running the Ben Race this year; nor did he run last year. It will take many of us a long time to get used to the idea of the Ben Race without Eddie. His death is a watershed in the history of the race: we have now entered the post-Eddie era.

No-one else comes close to matching his distinguished record in the Ben Race; first three times; in the top ten ten times; started and finished forty-four times; a continuous presence in the race from 1951 to 1995. He was as much a part of the race as the mountain itself.

Eddie, always a striking figure in his later years as befitted one who was different from the ordinary man, was a legend for his Ben Race exploits but there was a lot more to the man. He was inspirational to a host of runners both in Lochaber and in the wider world. Some top-class runners relied on Eddie's guidance when they attempted record-breaking runs on the Ben or other Lochaber mountains. His drive and resourcefulness led to a lot of new races entering the race calendar as a memorial to his energy and enthusiasm. We owe a lot to Eddie.

Essentially a modest man, he was still quietly confident of the work of his own achievements. This was what gave him serenity and dignity which characterised him. All of us who knew him felt privileged to do so. He had presence. In a sense, he still has. As a former Ben Race winner, Allan MacRae of Assynt wrote: "Eddie may be gone, but the challenge of the race remains. Other runners come and go, but Eddie has left an incredible mark on the history of the race."

Runners, remember Eddie at the summit cairn today; he was once tired and inspired as you.

Photos courtesy of Alex Gillespie

Dave O'Neil's elbow

A Verse on the Ben

Willie's Back

400 Hill Runners

Oh!
It's two o'clock and off we go along to Achintee

Chorus
Four hundred hill runners, all in front of me
Some take it oh so serious, some do it for a lark
I hope this year that I can make it back down to the park

My first year I was young, I didn't have a clue
Who was I to follow and what was I to do
I hid among the crowd and waited for my turn
And then I followed Brooksie, he went up the burn

Brooksie and Roger
(don't ask!)

My second I was fitter and thought I was in trim
I spotted Ronnie Campbell, and thought I'd follow him
He ran away and left me, I didn't see him for a while
Then I was passed by Ernie Orr jumping o'er the stile

I scratched my head with Willie, our old plans wouldn't do
This year I really think we needed something new
I raced that year with Dave O'Neil, who pushed me on the top
And Bodger ran so fast, I was sure that I would drop

Ernie Orr

The year I did beat Dodger he wasn't quite on form
This was '88 and the year of the storm
Johnny Maitland he was great and played it oh so cool
When he went charging past us, dressed up in a big cagoule

Robert Cant and Johnny Banks are always looking frisky
To run The Ben on such a day is always rather risky
Robert runs along the scree, with Johnny at his flank
He'd much prefer propping up the bar at Nevisbank

Johnny Banks

Billy Brooks caught me once way up on the scree
He wore a funny floppy hat, just the same as me
The marshals must have thought us mad we must have looked the fool
To dip them in the burn it was, to keep our hot heads cool

I had a friend called Callum we raced along together
Boulders were not quite his scene he'd rather have the heather
I shouted back my goodness whatever is the hurry
Do you not remember our wager man, we're racing for a curry

continued...

Johnny Maitland

A *Verse* on the Ben

Billy Brooks

The wise man of The Ben could only be but Eddie
Sprinting's not his scene so he likes to take it steady
The Walshes are not quite his thing he doesn't like the dash
So he is quite contented with a pair of old Green Flash

People came from far afield to run upon these races
The Finish Line it says it all it's written on their faces
I don't know why we do it but we'll do it once again
You'll never beat that classic race, the one they call The Ben

No you'll never beat
that classic race
The one
They call
THE BEN

Callum

David Rodgers
(Dodger)

Dave MacGillivray
(Bodger)

Ronnie Campbell

Robert Cant

John MacRae measuring his door to ensure there is room for his head to get in after he receives his "Connochie Plaque" for 21 Ben Nevis races – 2 more to go after the 2004 race. John had been hoping to do them all in under 2hrs but one hot year before the race he was supping away carefully to keep "hydrated", when he spied his pals taking that "isotope" stuff and had had a bottle. Just after the start he doubled up with stomach cramp and couldn't straighten up. He ran like this always hoping it would go away – it didn't. But anyway, one is bent most of the time going up! At the top however he still couldn't straighten and, in spite of his Quasimodo-like descent, he was still only 2hrs 30mins. Wow what an effort!

Gently does it...

...on the way down for Mary from Vancouver. She had avoided all the steep shortcuts on the descent but was still finding the loose going tricky. She had moved out to Canada in the 60s, but was always determined to return to climb The Ben to be upsides with her brother, who'd done it years ago – "He's older!" Mary said. He was at that moment in Skye, so it is nice Mary had a view of the island from the top.

Ever so gently does it...

...for Eric and Ann Robinson (no laughter please about being the same name as the stern presenter of the quiz show on TV, The Weakest Link, who has contestants quaking in their boots!). Eric and Ann are from Durham. They hadn't planned on doing The Ben, setting out to do a walk in Glen Nevis, but taking a wrong turning. They found themselves on the Ben Path and thought, "Go for it!" They pluckily reached the top but Ann's legs were at that jelly stage on the way down. Not far to go from here for that lovely hot bath! A loan of Mary's stick from the photo above would have been a big help to Ann. And so it was that I set about to find out just what benefit these sticks are – and spied a likely person to ask as she quick-marched past...

Georgina from Glasgow (below) was the one stepping it out and she paused long enough for a photo. By coincidence she was the perfect person to answer my questions about the walking poles as she had worked in the mountaineering shop, Graham Tiso's, in Glasgow... "20% reduction in strain on your knees plus the chance to steady yourself when you come down slippy places," she told me. Georgina was a competitive swimmer and is well used to all four limbs helping her along, 4x4 style. She didn't use the sticks on the way up, but they were a great boon on the descent. In all the old running pictures of early Ben Nevis races you will see most of the contestants with sticks, so Graham Brooks thought he'd reintroduce them – only to find himself on the horns of a dilemma... An Official informed him that if he ran with his sticks in the race, which was a counter for both the Scottish and the British Championship, then he would be disqualified from the Scottish section of the race. Graham ran and was well placed – minus his sticks!

As in every sport **"rules is rules"** and a very unfortunate disqualification happened to no lesser a person than Ben Maestro – the late Duncan MacIntyre (pictured right with Kathleen Connochie). Duncan was known as "The Butcher" more for his occupation than his manner on The Ben as he was a very gentle person, living and breathing the Ben Nevis Race right up to his death in 1987. I remember the distressing sight of Jim Peters attempting to finish the marathon in the 1954 Commonwealth Games and it was the same with poor Duncan while in the lead with just a hundred yards to go to the finish in the 1942 Ben Race. He collapsed to the ground and when his brother went to help him up, he was effectively disqualified from the race. The next year the race started and finished at the King George V Park rather than the High Street where he'd collapsed and Duncan came back to put it right – you wonder what was going through his head in those last hundred yards before breasting the tape! They didn't cry **"YES!"** and punch the air in those days!

And just who is Kathleen Connochie, the lady in white in the last photo alongside Duncan? Now there would be an ideal companion for your climb of The Ben, for in 1955 she set an unbeaten record of 3hrs 2mins. Nowadays, as Kate MacPherson, she restricts herself to handing out prizes rather than winning them as in the photo above. If you were to ask her nicely at an Old Time or Ceilidh dance, she might just chum you up The Ben! Kate had married another Ben Nevis Great, George MacPherson, for many years the Ben Nevis Race Association Secretary, who sadly died in 1991. Kate's father, Dr Connochie (below right) was a "Freeman" of Fort William and is remembered for his bow tie and the much sought after "Connochie Plaque" he donated to those doing 21 Ben Nevis races. The much-loved doctor, a founder member of the Race Committee, died in 1975 after 25 years service. Eddie had done his 21st Ben Race in 1971. Following in his father in law Eddie's footsteps, John Dugan got his plaque in 1999 so hasn't too many more years to do to be upsides with Eddie at 44 years! At present (that's after the 2004 race) there are 41 holders of the plaque. This is mine – although you'd hardly notice it so discreetly on the wall!

Inspired by a present of "The Munros"...

...from his father, Mark and Sue from Suffolk set off on a holiday to the Highlands and Islands. Mark said climbing The Ben was the highlight of their two weeks. 15 years ago he'd done Ben Lawers and both have climbed Snowdon and Scafell Pike. So to add The Ben brings them to this windy corner of the zigzags overlooking Five Finger Gully. Spoken about in hushed tones, the gully which plunges down into Glen Nevis, has claimed many lives.

One of those runners whose eyes lit up with fire whenever The Ben was mentioned, was such a victim – Peter Brooks.

On his 60th birthday, Peter had been doing one of his long mountain challenges – from the Cairngorms to Fort William. He had left The Ben to the last because, he said, **"As you know The Ben was very much part of my life over many years."** It was January 1998 and the simple but fatal slip occurred at the end of his journey. Peter was our spokesman on running affairs whenever there were microphones or press about – his business was PR! In his defence of expeditions which may sound foolhardy to some, Peter said, **"After all, it's a person to be pitied whose memories of fatigue and pain endured in the course of an arduous but pleasurable venture are not negated by the euphoria of the experience."**

No one could believe what befell the runner on the right, Ronnie Mackintosh... He is pictured here leaving the summit. Competitors arrived at the finish in ones and twos, but no Ronnie. Time went on and reports came in that he'd gone over Five Finger Gully! The Mountain Rescue rushed round into Glen Nevis and found him jogging along the road, shaken but not stirred. He had survived by running faster and faster from one tottery boulder to another to keep his balance, speed going up per second per second as he hurtled down the gully reaching about 40 mph!

Fortyfour plus three

A poem by Eddie

"I managed 44 + 3,
I enjoyed every one,
I hope you all do well today,
Even in the sun,
The aches and pains I'll miss today,
But you'll enjoy the bliss,
I know you'll all run well today
While I give it a miss"

"All the best."

Eddie encompasses **us all** with this wish – runners, walkers on the path, marshals, helpers and everyone who loves The Ben. But it wasn't Eddie who read out the poem over the tannoy to the hushed runners, it was announcer Rob Cameron. As we lined up for the start of the 1996 race, Rob explained that Eddie would not be here. He had only a few weeks to live and could not face coming to the park. To take his mind of it, he went to referee a shinty match instead!

The picture on the right, courtesy of Donald Mackay, is of Eddie officiating at the Camanachd Association's centenary shinty match at Kingussie in 1993.

The "+3" that Eddie refers to is three non-Ben Nevis Race Association runs on The Ben. The first being the cancelled race in 1980 when a few of us went up afterwards. The second event was that Eddie felt that the runners needed their annual fix of Ben running and so he held a "training run"(sic) a couple of weeks after. Roger Boswell won after a spectacular fall on the grassy slope in the Red Burn Gully. Certificates were given as a momento and here is John Dougan's:-

John is Eddie's son in law and he is pictured here (below left) running alongside "Santa" as we set off in the third of Eddie's extra races – The Centenary of the first Ben Nevis race. If you are puzzled why the runners are going away from The Ben, it was because we were looping round a marshal standing at the site of the Old Post Office in the High Street where the first race started. That marshal was none other than Kate Macpherson – Kathleen Connochie – without her lollypop!

LOCHABER AMATEUR ATHLETIC CLUB

This is to Certify that

John Dougan

did run and complete

the Ben Nevis Race course

on Sunday 21st September 1980

in **2** hours **15** minutes **57** seconds.

Signed *E Campbell*   Position **14**^TH

The runner in between Eddie and John in the photo on the top left is a faithful Ben campaigner, Tom O'Reilly (in white period costume). Tom hasn't changed much in the last hundred years! Tom was running against Eddie before Eddie had a beard! They had close tussles and became great friends.

"Above all," Tom wrote in Eddie's appreciation, *"Eddie was just a very nice person."*

The avuncular looking gentleman...

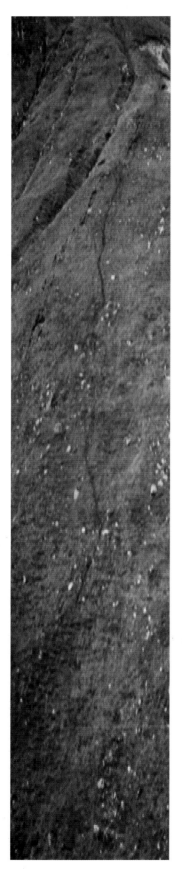

...in the middle is Alex Gillespie with wife Mary reaching the top in the Centenary Run. Meeting them at the cairn was Kenny Campbell, Eddie's son - not to be confused with Kenny (barrel organ) Campbell! In the 1978 Ben Nevis Race, Kenny had assisted Norman Bright, a blind American runner, to climb up and down. Norman suffered an arm injury along the way and was led over to the Red Cross tent at the finish by HRH the Duchess of Kent! Although not allowed to compete officially, Norman was given a rousing cheer when he ran down the aisle to collect a special award at the prize giving. Meanwhile, back at the Centenary Run, Roger Boswell and Jimmy Shields are approaching the top as Fiona Wild heads back down. I spoke to the pair as to why they were not leading the race, discovering they'd started late. Twins Jimmy (rearmost half) and Bobby (Ben winner in 1967) Shields are eyeing up an after race tea. So then I set off after Fiona's disappearing back. Round the corner I met Eddie, who, not thinking of his own struggles, told me to "look after Fiona." I never caught her! No wonder – when you see her go down the grassy slope...

Fiona flying down the Grassy Slope

Again not a thing to be tried at home, but it is a noted shortcut for the runners to come down the Red Burn screes to Halfway, then go straight over the pony track and dive down the Grassy Slope into the Red Burn Gully. In the days after the race you will see the track etched very clearly. Brooksie used this slope for "reps" going round by the halfway loch, then plunging down the 800 foot drop in under 3 minutes, then back up by the lochan again passing the same puzzled tourists 3 or 4 times! One runner shouted at him in the race, "Hoi, these shoes cost me £100 and you go zooming past on your bum!"

116

The long arm
of the law...

...became the long legs of the law, when it was realised that no one had been despatched to stop the traffic on Nevis Bridge. As this distinguished group made its way along from the King George V Park, the real leader was already out of shot... A policeman! He had come sprinting past clutching his hat! By the time we got to the bridge, he was calmly raising his hand to stop the cars. This is the 1969 race and the winner in his famous faded Reading vest was No 20, Mike Davies from Reading. Behind Eddie in the photo is No 147, Peter Colman of Vauxhall Motors, a Connochie Plaque holder. The Vauxhall running club were very keen on trying for records like the Three Peaks of Snowdon, Scafell Pike and The Ben. Eddie was always on hand to help their efforts. Notice the running shoes of the other runners – a move away from the canvas basketball style boots. Tom Weir, the great mountaineer and story teller, was observing the race in 1957 and noticed that the gym shoe shod runners went skating all over the place in the wet. Studs were the answer but some of us were slow to give up the old ways. Eddie's nickname was "The Green Flash Kid"! My own shoes at that time were a pair of Woolies black rubbers with a Commando sole welded on. Great grip, but heavy and the canvas gave way coming down the scree. A doctor on the hill was able to bind me up in a big bandage and I ran off down again with folk seeing the stookie and shouting that I should ease up. I just replied "'s OK, 's just my shoe!" Artist Ronnie Hope etched my basketball boots for ever in copper! In 1956 this same shoe trouble had happened to Brian Kearney when he was in the lead and he got a loan of tackety boots! Here is the transcript of a chat I had with him. He made the fifties come to life with his description of the races and the characters, bringing a whole new meaning of what before were just names of previous winners printed each year in the race programme...

"It's your day, Brian!"

It is time to introduce you to another Ben Nevis Icon – **Mr Brian Kearney** from Fort William, wearing No 31. Brian won The Ben Nevis Race three times and after his *"probably my best ever race,"* as he said, in 1957, he retired from running. He wanted to devote his time to other things like his love of sailing, but was still to be found untangling the strings for the runners on the summit every first Saturday in September until his recent heart problems. So it was, that with my recorder, I visited him in the Belford hospital. The nurse made "one minute" gestures so as not to tire him out and I found he'd been expecting me to call after he'd heard about the book! Straight away he started to reminisce...

The MacFarlane Cup being presented to Brian by Provost Macfarlane, who held the finishing tape. Brian was the first runner ever to break the 2 hour mark.

Brian proudly presents the MacFarlane Cup to Davy Rodgers, the first Fort William runner to win The Ben since Brian himself 34 years before.

"...when I lost the race through my own fault in 1956. I competed four times in it. You'll have heard of Pat Moy who was a tremendous runner. I mean he wasn't just an ordinary, he was an international runner. He represented Scotland many times. Well anyway, that particular time it was '56, I'd done the Three Peaks that time, that year – you know Snowdon, Scafell. We broke the existing record. Anyway I remember that day – it was a nice day. Pat, he wasn't so good at coming down but he was excellent going up. I says "Och, I'll let him he go, he'll not keep the thing up. But the boots I had, that was a problem with me – footwear. Now I could show you a picture of some basketball boots. They weren't baseball, they were basketball boots. Now my brother was in the RAF at the time and he saw these boots – they were heavy. There were special cushioned insoles in them. They were heavy going up, but were great for coming down like the stones, you know? Now I had them from 1951 to 1956. I used to come in at night and my father said "You're putting these beside the fire and the canvas is getting worn." he said. Not meaning to make excuses, quite genuine because the story's never been elaborated on, but anyway I didn't worry about it, but they were £6 a pair! Now that was a week's wages in the '50s. It's a lot, so I said "Ach!" but my father warned me - he said, "get yourself a new pair of boots." So anyway, Pat got a tremendous lead and I realised I'd better catch him up because he was getting too much of a lead. He was excellent going up but he wasn't good at coming down. So I was catching him no bother on the way down and I was just above the halfway house, just got off the scree and there was so much pressure at the side off the boots, this one came out the side,

The much sought after canteen of cutlery (bottom right of photo) is still on Brian's side-board!

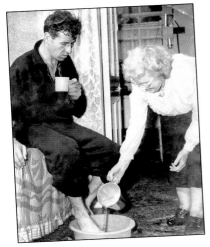

I see Brian has won the cup again!

then it came out the other side! I sat down – what am I going to do? I knew I couldn't go any further, but who come into sight but Eddie and then the fellow, Stan Horn. Two excellent runners as you know, and Eddie shouts to me, we were St Mary's, "Borrow a pair of boots from somebody!" because we wanted to win the team race as well. So there was a Councillor, Sauchie MacKay and his son who were sitting just below the halfway house – he was sitting with a pair of hobnailed boots! I tore these off – I tried to run so far, but you couldn't in bare feet. So he lent me his tackety boots and I finished fourth. I was raging at myself for being so stupid. I always remember coming into the park and the young boy, he must have had a bicycle, because next thing he's tapping me, he says "My father wants his boots to get off The Ben!" So that was it, but there was a wee bit of controversy about who would have won it. Pat said he would have beaten me. He said I would have beaten him on the hill all right, he said he'd have beaten me on the flat. But we were the best of friends. You know how they say "well, you've had it – forget that, just a local boy against an international runner, don't really lose sight of the fact!" But anyway at the Cairngorm race, I got my revenge and I beat him on the flat!"

A lovely story Brian told me was of the late Jimmy Conn, another great Ben runner. They'd been in Arran at the Goatfell race in 1957 and Brian had left before the prize giving because he was embarrassed about people seeking his autograph. Jimmy had said he'd collect Brian's certificate and get it to him – which Jimmy duly did when he visited Brian in hospital three years ago! The yellowing certificate was getting on for fifty years old! Luckily there wasn't an Arran Cheese as you get now! In an after race get-together in the Palace Hotel, the Olympic Great – the late Chris Brasher, who'd started the race and presented the prizes, had to take a back seat while Brian signed autographs. Brian apologised to him and that was when Chris said, *"It's your day, Brian!"*

One sight that would have been worth seeing was when Brian found an ice axe as the snow melted, and he came charging down the scree brandishing it... "You look like a warrior!" his running companion, Hughie Cameron had said.

An elderly man called to see Brian one day and introduced himself as Danny Mulholland, holder of the record from 1939. Danny sat and made the early days come alive – the way Brian has made the 50s for me. **A lot of history in one man!**

Photos courtesy of Brian's collection

Two Stalwarts

Photo courtesy of Alex Gillespie

Ben *and* Nevis

Which is which? It'll take a few moooooments to decide, but no trip to The Ben is complete until you have a photo of these two at the Ben Nevis Distillery on the main Inverness road at Lochybridge just as you leave Fort William going north. By popular demand, the pair have been joined by a family now, so you will be able to see a "Hielan' Beastie" calf. *"Up The Ben wi' Eddie"* is full of handy hints and here's another one – **don't** climb the fence to get your photo taken beside them! But **do** go into the Distillery – even if only to see the great display of Ben Nevis memorabilia!

The Distillery is the starting point of another path up The Ben, which is mainly used by climbers heading for the C.I.C. hut, nestling at the foot of the North Face cliffs. This hut is a private bothy owned by The Scottish Mountaineering Club and built in memory of climber Charles Inglis Clark. The route follows the Allt a' Mhuilinn burn and was the way Clement Wragge went up to take his weather readings before the Pony Track was built. One person who goes up in Clement's footsteps early October each year, is John Pottie. It is John's brief to clamber up the screes from the C.I.C. hut and measure the remnants of the snow bank in Observatory Gully, which is always the last to melt. He ran in the Ben Nevis Race in 1999 and surprised the summit marshals by running on past them and climbing up the cairn to the trig point! Another connection John has with our story is that he was the person who designed the Glen Nevis Visitor Centre with its lovely pillars.

A misty day on the top of The Ben in September, contrasted with a nice sunny February day in the Pentlands for the Carnethy hill Race where the photo is of John

warming up before the start. Eddie Campbell was a great supporter of the Carnethy and for years the race could boast of having at least six Ben Nevis winners running every time! Talking of Ben winners - with the Ben Nevis Race Association offering the £1000 to whoever breaks the male and female record, the committee thought to invite the record holders to come up for the 2004 race and be put up in the luxurious Alexandra Hotel. The Treasurer was highly delighted when he heard that Kenny Stuart and Pauline Haworth were man and wife! Will the 20-year-old record be broken? The top half of The Ben isn't as easy to run down nowadays, unless you take a leaf out of Big Jock Petrie's book… This tale of very "derring-do" happened when the Melantee pipes were being constructed. Jock Petrie was a larger than life figure and he was working on the Aluminium Works construction. One day his mates said that you Ben Nevis runners aren't so tough – Jock snatched his shovel and jumped into the top of one of the pipes and emerged

seconds later at the foot in a shower of sparks! He was a great favourite of Mrs Hobbs of Inverlochy Castle and she had a special prize of a silver bowl for Jock as the oldest entrant at 48 in the 1951 race. What a line-up of characters!

Back row: Eddie, Brian Kearney and brother Tommy, Jock himself, Charlie Sim, Duncan MacIntyre, Archie MacLachlan.
Front row: Alec MacDonald, Allan MacLean, Jock's sons, Charlie and Allan, Allan Grant, M. Reavie.

The Ben Nevis Express

Phew! Following that emotional draining on the left, Allan Petrie sat back in his favourite chair after reliving the Golden Era of the fifties, wife Nan ready with a cup of hot sweet tea! For with Allan's descriptions we had been leaping across the ravines before all the bridges were reinstated *("a distance which would have beaten the Olympic long jump record!")*, flashing down the screes which in the early days started above Black Rock, over the side of which they hurtled, and skidding down the grassy slope with one hand out behind like a rudder! *"You felt you could do anything!"*

Allan's brother Charlie (on right of Eddie) returned from Canada on holiday and entered the Ben Race in 1971 and is shaking hands with Eddie – nineteen years on from having been second to Eddie in 1952! Allan was 6th and, with Jimmy Conn in 3rd place, they won the team prize – Eddie running for St Mary's and the lads running for the Ben Nevis Athletic Club in the pre-Lochaber Athletic Club days. L.A.C.'s first Ben was in 1957 getting 1st team.

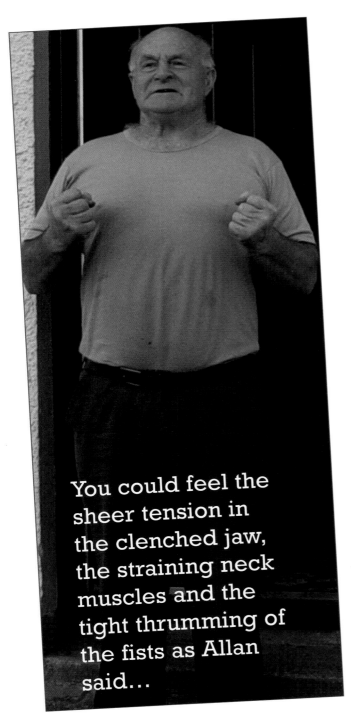

You could feel the sheer tension in the clenched jaw, the straining neck muscles and the tight thrumming of the fists as Allan said…

"You felt like a bunch of springs!"

The Tartan Terrors!

In that 1952 race, Charlie on the left with Allan on the right and the late Jimmy Conn in the middle made up the very first team to win Mrs Hobbs' team trophy with silver medals and plaques (now gold medals).

Allan was remembering it was a wet, cold day with a blizzard on the top (18th June 1952) and an attempt was made to have radio coverage for the race. A team of horses was coaxed up to the top carrying all the gear and, while those who toiled up with them had a cuppa in the shelter of the old Observatory, the horses did what horses do – they rolled on their backs with their loads! So no broadcasts that year, but the following year the Lovat Scouts were up and running and relayed an important message from the summit judges that they would not be able to survive the weather without a drop of the "Cratur". Their lives were not in the balance for long, because off shot a runner with 2 bottles of brandy, reached the top and was back in time for the start! Duncan MacIntyre!

One competitor was a long long time coming into the park after being sighted at Nevis Bridge and was found to have stopped in at the Nevis Bank Hotel for a reviver, then went on to win a length of cloth for a suit!

Plenty of these above names deserve the title on the last page of "Ben Nevis Express", but Allan told me of one of the Ben phenomena...

Big Jock Petrie on his way to find his silver rose bowl he got from Mrs Hobbs in '51 – It disappeared mysteriously when Charlie emigrated to Canada!

The Glen Nevis Express

Not a superhuman one, but a natural one – a wind which comes from nowhere, whistles across by the Esso Station and disappears just as quick. Allan has experienced it once and all you can do is lie flat – Allan told me it struck the BA factory by flattening their steel mesh boundary fence and sent caravans and huts 40ft in the air. I have heard mention of buttons being snatched off the coats of the pipeline workers. Fine to have a cut down version of the Express at your back going up so long as it dies away when you get near the cliffs at the top! Allan once had a brush with the cliffs when he was going up the Red Burn screes in a "pea-souper". He got a funny feeling all was not well and slowed right down to a crawl just in time to find himself from here to the fireplace from the 2,000ft drop down the North Face!

A young Eddie crosses the finishing line to win the 1952 race. Eddie's comment of the dreadful conditions was "Nine starters retired (a wise decision on their part)."

Posted Missing

In 1955, while Eddie was winning the race and Kathleen Connochie was setting her record, a drama was unfolding on The Ben which only came to light for me in October '04. I received a phone call to meet a Mr Gil (for Gilbert) Calder at the Torvean Golf Course in Inverness (photos 1980 & 2004). I was searching the room for likely looking ex-Ben runners when in came Gil with Hugh Dan's "The Ben Race" book under his arm. We read the passage about G. Calder being "roundly ticked off" for not reporting to the nearest official that he'd retired from the race after getting lost in the mist after halfway. Then Gil explained just what had occurred that "dry with light wind, misty on summit" day almost 50 years ago...

Although entered as Inverness, his home town, Gil had done most of his hill and track running whilst at Markinch in Fife. He came up to try The Ben without knowing the best route and mistake number one came when he ran up the grassy slope to the Red Burn Crossing at Halfway – a total energy drainer! By the time he entered the mist in the Red Burn screes, he was completely on his own and, after ages of clambering up and up, he was aware that the ground was now sloping down! Time for that prickly feeling and in talking afterwards to a police sergeant it became clear he had come to the edge of the North West face! *"He marked out where I was and according to him I was standing on the North West face at the time. Apparently - I've never been up – there's cairn markers going along the NW face. I had actually gone to one of them and gone between them and advanced to the edge almost dangling a foot over. You felt like continuing as if you had to jump a yard and you'd land on the other side. Every time I called out I heard a voice, seeming to be from my right, calling back – was it just an echo? When I tried to go to my right, this ledge just seemed to come right round in front of me. So I put my back to that and went back towards the cairn and I always remember (the only time I ever experienced it) a cold shiver went right through me. I don't know if it went up the way or down the way – and just as if a voice spoke to me and said "You're*

lost!" and everything seemed to change from that second onwards. My thoughts of completing the race had completely gone. My thoughts were of survival to get back down. So I wandered about up there for a while. Felt like resting – a good job I didn't.

[Just to interrupt Gil's story at this point... 2 years after, in 1957, a runner lost a shoe in the Red Burn screes and crawled behind a boulder to rest – here is how Eddie described what happened:- "Sadly one of the competitors, John Rix from Surrey, lost a shoe in the Red Burn and took shelter behind a rock. He was found by a search party later that night but died from exhaustion as he was being stretchered down the mountain. This cast a deep gloom over the future of Ben Nevis running but his many close friends knew that he would have been the last person to want the Ben Race stopped."]

Gil at last saw a dim shape going past in the mist and headed for it, regaining the small pebbles of the path. He came on a marshal who said thank goodness that he'd been found and just to go for a shower and the marshal would mark him in. Gil went home after his shower at the Aluminium Works not knowing the marshal had forgotten to register him as retired. He was completely unaware of the black mark that has remained against his name from then till now. I told Gil it was a shame he hadn't gone to the after race dance as Kathleen Connochie had bumped into her future husband going in the door – it might just have been him!

And now they will meet... Both Gil and Kathleen are in my relay team, Kathleen reprising her role with a photo-shoot on the same stile as fifty years ago and Gil to breast the tape at the finish! The relay race is a bid to "Beat the hour for Eddie" up and down The Ben from Claggan Park. The fund-raising event will not take place until 3rd July '05 when conditions are more "user friendly" on the mountain, but we need the money now! "Not exactly the Corinthian spirit," said Leen Volwerk of the Ben Nevis Race Association! One thing sure 'though – it will be a lot of fun!

Here is our "Up The Ben wi' Eddie" group gathered round the handsome award certificate of £5000 of lottery funding.

Left to right in the photo by Iain Ferguson are front row: Graham Brooks, JJ, Eddie's widow

Chrissie Campbell, Sharon Smith and back row: Jim Smith (winner of the lovely painting of The Ben's NW face, donated by local artist and climber, David Wilson, shown with picture on the right), John Macdonald, John MacRae. Missing from the group picture in Sharon's Cancer Research shop due to pressure of work are Peggy Rose and Ken Johnston (pictured left). Laughing fit to bust, beside Peggy in the left hand photo, is Margaret MacLean, to whom I was talking on the phone below the helicopter in the Lorna story – getting her lines crossed again!

Colonel Dawson's dog is sloping off before a rope gets attached to its collar!

"I want a Champ on top of The Ben!"

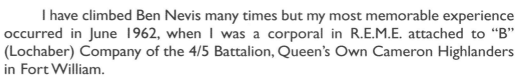

Thus spake the Battalion Commander, but he wasn't meaning running – he wanted his men to help the recruitment drive by taking an Austin Champ up to summit. Here is the driver Willie Stirling's gripping story as he wrote in "Lochaber Life" with exciting pictures of how it came to pass...

About 800ft (ascent)

I have climbed Ben Nevis many times but my most memorable experience occurred in June 1962, when I was a corporal in R.E.M.E. attached to "B" (Lochaber) Company of the 4/5 Battalion, Queen's Own Cameron Highlanders in Fort William.

Our company commander, Major Roddy MacGregor was approached by Col. Dawson, battalion commander, to "put a 'Champ' on top of Ben Nevis" to attract attention to an army recruitment drive.

The Austin Champ was a cross-country vehicle similar in size to a Land Rover and fitted with a Rolls Royce engine. It had four-wheel drive, independent suspension all round and weighing 34 cwt was much heavier than the Land Rover.

About 1000ft
Capt R. MacDonald

I was entrusted with the vehicle preparation and after some careful reconnaissance and planning of the route, we were ready to go on Friday 8th June. The party of 16 left the Drill Hall at 7.30 p.m., and with myself driving we approached the Ben through the Ben Nevis Distillery. Crossing the moor, we got on to the BA Light Railway which we followed for about half a mile. From that point, we started up the hill and by nightfall had reached about 1000 feet and camped there for the night.

We woke at 6 a.m. to find it raining and misty. Undeterred, and with the honour of the company at stake, we struggled upwards through the bogs, reaching the Lochan by lunchtime.

Red Burn Crossing
(no longer like this!)

We joined the main track below the Red Burn and after crossing the burn the going was a bit easier, apart from the hairpin corners, which proved difficult. We reached the fifth hairpin at about 4.30 and discovered we had misjudged the Champ's thirst for fuel, when it ran out of petrol.

We returned down the hill, and early on the Sunday, we carried 20 gallons of petrol up to the Champ, got going again, and reached the summit by 5.30 p.m. It was a very satisfying moment for the whole team, who had worked so hard.

About 3000ft
Major MacGregor

Snow on the last lap to the summit

The 'team' on the summit

Parked on the summit

On the last half-mile to the summit we had to contend with fairly deep snow and due to the fact that the foot-brake had ceased to function because of a fluid leak, it was decided to leave the vehicle on the summit and return the following weekend. We left it parked between the trig point and the Observatory and hid the equipment.

The next Saturday afternoon, a few of us went up. I got the brake working and we slept the night in the climbers' shelter.

On the Sunday morning, the rest of the team arrived to assist in the descent, and we were back in the Drill Hall by 4.30.

We had taken about 16 hours driving time on the ascent and 5½ hours coming down.

Our equipment was primitive but effective, consisting of 4 steel channels, 2 ground anchors and 2 pulley blocks, with about 100 yards of rope. The Champ was none the worse for the experience and the battalion and company commanders praised our teamwork and commitment to the task.

Near Red Burn
(descent)

PS. Willie can't stop after a lifetime of service to the motor trade and can now be found at the Inverlochy cycle shop. He knew George Simpson well, the man who drove the Baby Austin up to the top. Willie was approached by Ford to advise on getting their latest model, the Escort, up for the 50th anniversary of Henry Alexander's climb, but this was stopped in case of accident. An Austin Gypsy got to the summit a fortnight before the Champ — but it wasn't a race!

"Doon the Ben"

My own little "claim to fame" came in August 1974, but this would have been totally eclipsed by well-known climber and rescuer Alex Howie (in photo) and his friend Billy Munro. The two of them had been climbing The Ben via the North-east Buttress and had come over the rim at the top of the cliffs and onto the summit plateau. Their route to go down by the Pony Track took them past the ruins of the Observatory. It was a chilly misty day and they had no wish to linger at the top, so along they went, heads bent as they concentrated on their direction. Alex started to get the feeling he was being watched and turned towards the vague outline of the deserted buildings. Every hair on Alex's head stood bolt upright when he saw soundless figures in old fashioned tweeds waving their long Victorian walking sticks! He looked away and then looked again, hoping nothing would be there. Ah, but there was! Hazy shapes that drifted in and out of vision. Alex turned to his friend, "Em, Billy, Do you see what I see?"

"Yes!" was all Billy had time to say before the pair of them were heading down for Achintee at the toot!

The thought of a "vision" inspired my saga of "Familiar Squat Cairns" and I am very lucky to have newly retired from Lochaber High School, art teacher Alistair Smyth doing his unique illustrations for me…

DOWN BEN NEVIS IN 23 MINUTES

A race from the summit of Ben Nevis to the foot of the mountain was held for the first time on Sunday and was won by Jim Jardine, Midlothian, in a time of 23 minutes. Second was Bobby Shields, Clydesdale Harriers, and local veteran Eddie Campbell came third.

The event attracted 14 runners. Each was sent off from the top at half-minute intervals.

"Every hair on Alex's head stood bolt upright"

It was raining in Fort William. Figures hurried along the High Street past the hotel. Inside, in his usual corner, with slumped shoulders, sat the once proud victor of a long forgotten race. The centenary hype of one hundred years of Ben Nevis Running was passing him by until, later that night, it was all to change...

Part One – The Challenge

Downstairs in the Grand, with a pint in his hand,
An Englishman looked over, choking,
"What, him in the shirt – that little squirt?
You've really got to be joking."

He pushed through the crowd and shouted out loud,
"Last of the great record men!
I'll bet you, old sonny, any amount of money,
I could beat you down The Ben.

I've won the Nevis Race at a new record pace.
No one can run like I do.
I've won every event from here down to Kent,
Now I want your record too."

Staring into my drink, I started to think,
"Why couldn't I answer the clown?
If I swallowed my fear like I swallowed my beer;"
But no – I could only look down.

"Can't run, can't jive – now can't even drive…"
I heard him continue to jeer.
"I'm not surprised he was breathalysed –
He can't even hold his beer.

Looks as old as the hills and rattles with pills,
With a face like an old worn-out shoe.
Imagine him on a date! If he ever found a mate,
I doubt if he'd know what to do."

A different voice spoke – a local sounding bloke,
"Ah now, I think there was something.
For I've heard that he keeps a wee box where he sleeps,
And in it, some say, is a ring."

"A RING!" he still raged, "So our friend was engaged.
What on earth to d'you suppose?
What sort of old cow would wear his ring now,
Unless perhaps going through her nose!"

The table and chair went up in the air,
As I leapt up and glared in his face.
"Tomorrow at ten, at the top of The Ben,
I'll give you your downhill race."

Part Two – The Race

He was drawing away at a terrible speed,
Nothing I could do would shorten his lead.
His shape became vaguer, then faded from view.
His steps became softer, then disappeared too.

"What, him
in the shirt?"

"Last of
the great
record men!"

"The table and chair
went up in the air"

Off the summit plateau, the wind lost its force,
My feet soon thawed out on their zigzagging course.
My hands and my body started getting warm,
And on the smooth scree banks, I clicked into form.
Familiar Squat cairns would loom up like friends,
Their yellow dye markings would show me the bends.

Part Three – The Decision

John MacInnes, the Inspector, always finishes a lecture,
With something that I was to learn:
At this time of year, huge holes will appear,
Just under the snow on Red Burn.

If a man were to slip, he could rip off his hip,
But he was now so far below,
To have any chance at all, I must risk the fall,
So I swung off the track - to the snow.

Part Four – The Vision

Sound and horizon now all seemed to go,
As I hurtled down over that thin crust of snow.
Twenty to thirty miles an hour I'd be reaching,
Trying to shut out any thoughts of a breaching.
"JIMMY!" Like a needle a voice pierced my brain;
I slowed down and stopped when I heard it again.
A blue-shimmering form was waving to me,
But against the bright whiteout, I just couldn't see.
The vision now faded, but I knew who she was,
And when I looked down, I soon saw the cause –
A jagged hole had opened to the Red Burn below,
And her warning had saved me from death in the snow!
Back to full speed, I was soon at halfway,
And out from the clouds to a beautiful day.
Look away down Loch Eil to the Cuillins of Skye,
But it wasn't the view that was catching my eye…
It was the sight of the Englishman at "Broken Bridge" –
He was walking! He was walking down the ridge.
I passed him at the deer fence, but he didn't see me,
He flaked out on the road when he reached Achintee.

Part Five – The Finish

With each step my hate had begun to abate,
Even with Fort William in view.
Inside I'd a glow, and just seemed to know
That she'd have forgiven him too.

I swung round again and went back to The Ben,
Helping him up to his feet.
Back down at the Grand, he lifted his hand,
Toasting the result – a dead heat.

"Nothing I could
do would shorten
his lead"

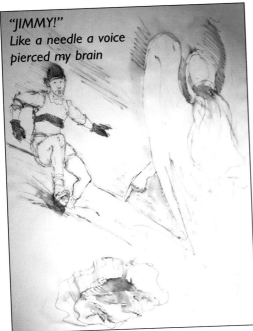

"JIMMY!"
Like a needle a voice
pierced my brain

"- a dead heat."

"Gentlemen Songsters
off on a spree!"

Photos courtesy of Noel Williams who escorted the choir up by coincidence their conductor was also a Noel (Noel J.M. Lee). The Gentlemen Songsters are from Dudley and had Bert Bissell as their President. This is them in 1978, becoming the first choir to scale the heights - they have also plumbed the depths, performing in the "Chunnel" and a Devonshire cavern (Kent Cavern)! Noel received a signed copy of their LP. The choir did an encore in 1997 on top of The Ben when laying a wreath at the Peace Cairn on behalf of Bert Bissell who was in Fort William viewing his favourite Ben before he died aged 96 the following year.

"Where the snow flake reposes!"

Definitely in with the bricks is Noel the geologist!

Noel in the '96 Ben Nevis Race

After a trip down the Red Burn screes, you sometimes find the stones in your running shoes don't "settle" and you have to stop to empty them – little chips of different colours depending on how high you are up The Ben. It is a bit like changing a wheel after a puncture and I thanked a mother and daughter for a nice little round of applause following a swift pit stop. Noel always makes the unique geology of Ben Nevis a talking point when taking visitors up the Pony Track and puts into easy terms where the four main rocks are on The Ben...

1. **Metamorphics** (at Achintee)
2. **Outer Ben Nevis Granite with dykes** (from the stile until just before the Halfway Lochan).
3. **Inner Ben Nevis Granite** - redder in colour from the outer (from halfway – including the Red Burn Crossing – to the Third Zigzag)
4. **Volcanic lavas etc** – grey in colour (from Third Zigzag to the summit)

Noel got his Connochie Plaque in 2001 for completing 21 Bens. He is the author of "Scrambles in Lochaber".

Noel says he finds it fascinating that the highest rocks in the country sank many hundreds of feet to reach their present position – see next page!

Many of the large rocks on The Ben have names and it is interesting to find out their history. Clement Wragge took readings at the Livingston Boulder, approaching half way from the north. When Hugh Dan MacLennan was researching his Ben Nevis Race book, he decided to climb the path and see for himself the famous landmarks such as "Clint's Rock", on the right hand side of the Pony Track up from Eddie's Bench. It used to have the former path worker's name emblazoned on but is now washed off. Local guides knew to stand away from certain stones on the summit when taking bearings in bad weather because of their iron content – one thought is that they may have come from outer space! What a good excuse for doing badly in the race – "I was goin' great till I got struck by a meteor!"

One rock not to even think of approaching is "Frenchie's Pinnacle" and I had played it down on the Clitheroe page in the hope no one would be tempted to try it! Noel, member of the Lochaber Mountain Rescue Team, said he had a bit of trouble persuading his friend Frenchie Cameron on the pinnacle to take his hand off the wall to his left! ! Rocks have names traditionally given to them over the centuries from the mists of time – like Samuel's Stone (above) in Glen Nevis on the way to the Visitor Centre. This rock has the power to grant you three wishes *if*, and I'm afraid it's a big *if*, you encounter the 50-ton stone spinning.

*Characters have names too – like **"Poiken"** for the late Donald MacDonald, a real Ben race enthusiast. Poiken recounts in his booklet Glen Nevis/Ben Nevis when Samuel's Stone was shifted to its present location to make way for the new road, the driver "experienced a strange and eerie sensation" and left the job!*

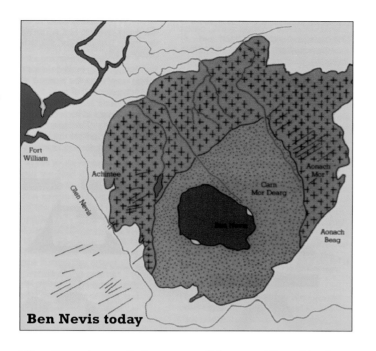

Ben Nevis today

GRANITE / DYKE \ GRANITE

**Dyke in outer granite on Ben Path
(above youth hostel)**

The 4 main rock types making up Ben Nevis

Lava   Schist   Outer granite   Inner granite   Dykes

Collapse of Ben Nevis Summit
Four hundred million years ago

STAGE 1: Volcano erupts and lava flows into lake. Magma from outer granite (pink) is intruded in underground chamber.

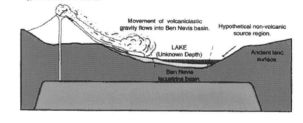

STAGE 2: Dykes are injected, then magma of inner granite (orange) is intruded.

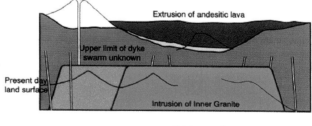

STAGE 3: Cauldron roof collapses and down comes the entire mass above to get stuck like a bung. The Ben as we know it today is formed when the rest erodes away.

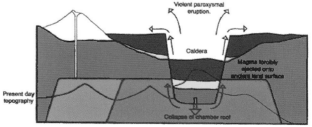

The summit today

(Thanks to Noel Williams for info and photo – the 3 steps to collapse diagrams are by Rod Burt, who went off to study volcanoes in New Zealand)

I got a shock...

Photo courtesy of Roger Boswell

...looking down from the Pony Track onto a shock of tight white curls coming up a short cut, body stripped to the waist — it was just like Eddie, photographed here at the finish of "Tranter's Round". With Eddie in the photo is George Smith, who died so cruelly in a fall on Beinn Fhionnlaidh in Argyll in March '04. The owner of the hair in fact had been a running friend of Eddie's and has a huge part in the history of Ben Nevis — Ken "Jono" Johnson, the writer of the "Dear Editor" letter about the Rangers. Ken of the Lossiemouth Mountain Rescue Team provided me with 2 hour's worth of tales of adventure on The Ben, but you won't see his name writ large, as he is a very private person. He would only appear in reports as *"a naval spokesman said…"*. That included epic rescues such as the four submariners where 2 were killed and one went on to marry his nurse at the old Belford Hospital. It is typical of Ken that after stringing all the Mamores, Grey Corries and The Ben Group together in a round to be done in under 24 hours (Ken did it in 22!), he encouraged Philip Tranter to call it "Tranter's Traverse". It was the same story for guidebooks but most authors did give credit to those like Ken who'd written and climbed the routes before.

Ken prizes, most of all, his friends of old and when standing at his window overlooking The Ben and Glen Nevis, he can remember the days spent with those still here and those gone. Ken let me read the eulogy to his late friend Norman Tennant and I was laughing out loud at Norman being so forthright… *When asked if he took sugar in his coffee, he replied "Not if it is good coffee", took a theatrical sip then asked for two spoonfuls of sugar!*

Malcolm Slessor, the climber and author, keeps Ken up to date with his trips with photos from all over the world — *"this is me on the glacier"*. Malcolm was awarded the Mungo Park Medal of the Royal Scottish Geographical Society and Mungo Park the explorer himself was one of the very earliest climbers of The Ben to be followed by "The fattest woman in the whole of Inverness-shire"! History repeated itself 100 years later when Ken was taking a large party up The Ben and came across a very stout lady in her seventies making her way up, lightly clad and shod and carrying two Tesco bags. Up and down went Ken mustering his big group and keeping a watchful eye on the lady as well. Her look on reaching the summit was as if she'd walked into a fabulous Cathedral! Delivering his lot safely down, Ken went back up to encourage his new charge. He reckons he did about five Bens that day!

Navy Ken enjoyed good healthy inter-services rivalry with the late John Hinde of RAF Kinloss. On returning up Glen Nevis after being "on the tiles" Ken spied Fiona, the Kinloss mascot, and had always nurtured a yearn to kidnap her. Fiona had other ideas and, being a goat, rammed him in the middle. Down went Ken on his back with a huge rucksack and, like a stranded turtle, rocked himself gently to sleep! He at last captured her at Aviemore and fed her tatties and veg at Glenmore till a very angry John arrived!

Ken pointing to the ice axes — what stories each one could tell! There is a "stop press" addition to "20 Yrs on Ben Nevis" where Wm Kilgour tells of the Rev. Robertson being hurled unconscious down 2,000ft in the snow on The Ben after his ice axe was struck by lightning, losing his cap!

How to eke out your holiday money...

1. Mountain Craft

It was perfect – rain and wind lashed the streets of Fort William. It would be sleet halfway up the Ben. Good! The windows of McTavish's Kitchen were steamed up. Excellent! It would have lessened the impact of my arrival if they'd seen me get out of a car.

I parked the car up the side lane and quickly jumped out. I undid my cagoule from the roof rack – the outside was nicely sodden. Fine! I put it on. A trickle of water ran down my neck. I hadn't bargained for that. Just hope I don't catch a cold, that's all!

I pushed open the swing door and went in. At the swish of the door, heads turned. I had their attention.

"Grim up the Ben!" I announced loudly, dripping pools of water beside the nearest table.

"Pleeze?" they enquired.

I summoned up all my linguistic powers, raising my voice **"UP ZEE BEN DE NEVIS."**

They understood at last.

"Yes thanks, I will have a cup of tea – two sugars please. Cumpick? Oh you mean camping! No, I was RUNNING!"

Again the heads turned and I acknowledged with a modest nod.

"I'll say it was cold. The only thing that kept me going was the vision of a steaming plateful of cottage mince and chips. Oh thank you – with peas please. Where's the brown sauce? You want to climb the Ben? Well, basically the mountain is shaped like a giant chocolate puddin'... Thank you, don't mind if I do!"

Cartoon by Bill Bentall

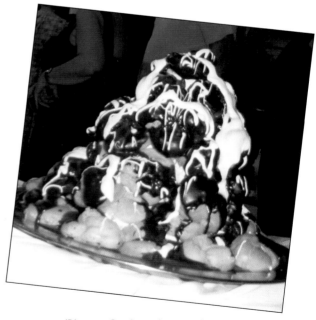

(Photo of cake taken on Jane and my Scottish Country Dancing holiday to Cyprus, Jan '04, just before we got stuck into it!)

The *Last Laugh*

*by Richard Gorman
of Westerlands CCC*

The Gormans are a real running family - Richard's 21st Ben Nevis race was in 1997. Richard's son Manuel is pictured running through the pages of his report on an epic 112 Munros from Ben Hope, the most northerly, to Ben Lomond the most southerly. Manuel's wife Lesley is pictured (in the pink) below in a post race "ceilidh" which can be fiercer than the actual event!

They come to Fort William to run up the Ben,
Those wild mountain women and mad mountain men.
Bum bag to the rear and best Walsh to the fore,
To do it just once and THEN NEVER NO MORE!

Carry full body cover in hail, rain or shine
And if you don't have it you don't cross the line.
Then once round the park at a suicide pace
- till the dips in the road take the smile off your face.

Past Achintee and up over the stile,
All the bellows are working hard in single file.
Scramble up between levels of path where you must
- by the wee metal bridge, all the bellows are bust.

The clouds have all parted, it's sunny and clear;
Was T-shirt and Lifa a clever idea?
Forget about running – you're starting to toil;
If it gets any hotter you'll feel your blood boil.

Plod on round the shoulder, the burn down below;
Should someone get past you then just let him go.
And enjoy a smug smile knowing that he
Will be totally knackered when he hits the scree.

The dyke, wade the burn, the mud field's a slog;
The climb by the lochan's a vertical bog
That drags on your Walshes and doubles their weight
- but they'll soon be washed clean, by the Red Burn in spate.

Slip and slide up the gravel without any grip
And you've scarcely enough of your sweat left to drip;
With your hands on your knees and your tongue at your feet,
Do you put your cagoule on – or suffer the sleet?

Three thousand feet gone and a thousand to go
- but the boulders and stones look much nicer in snow;
And now when you no longer could outrun a snail,
You can not get a breath in that damned force ten gale.

The summit at last! As the hail starts to sting
You nearly strangle yourself with that wee bit of string
That the marshal requires before he can say
You did make it up there – on at least the right day.

And now the climb's over, descending's a breeze
- if you can only ignore the gross pain in you knees,
If your stitch goes away and your ankles don't twist
When the blind man you followed gets lost in the mist.

Made it clear of the scree - and you still have some skin;
There's a drunk up ahead and you're pulling him in;
But you quickly discover just why his brain's numb,
As you slide down THE GREEN WALL and lose half your bum.

The mud chute, THE RED BURN, a short climb and you're out.
"HERE COMES A RUNNER!" the spectators shout.
So you step to the side to let him come through
- then hide your surprise, when you find they mean you.

The shoulder, the steel bridge, the track to the stile;
You're flying it now heading for the last mile.
Till you hit the road with an agonised groan,
To discover your legs have ideas of their own.

With your right twitching left, and your left folding right,
You'll be doing well if you finish tonight;
And the mob that you beat on the hill to get clear
Have all gone charging past like they're smelling free beer.

But just dig deep once more, then into the park,
Sprint round and you'll finish before it gets dark,
Fall over the line as your legs start to buckle
- and listen real hard; can't you hear EDDIE chuckle…?

"- and listen real hard; can't you hear EDDIE chuckle…?"

"*Will the last person to leave Ben Nevis kindly turn out the lights*"

Donna went ahead and set light sticks for Charlie to follow in the dark

There is a good Ben Nevis ghost story by Ken Crocket called "The Path" in which climbers, out in the worst of conditions, are nearly perishing when a light shows them the way. However Donna's lights are real and light the way through the rain, sleet and snow for this story of real endeavour by Charlie Anderson.

Everything got so sodden that Charlie had to call in the expertise of John MacRae's money laundering service!

First there came *"The Three Peaks"*, then there was *"Ramsay's Round"* and now there is a completely new challenge - *"The Charlie Anderson"*! **The number of times you can go up and down The Ben in 24 hours.** How Eddie would have loved it! He would have been preparing schedules, arranging supporters and becoming totally immersed in it. It had actually been done before Eddie started out on his Ben career – by none other than Jock Petrie, who did three times in 24 hours in the 1940s, but it didn't catch on! Jock, as you'll notice in his photos throughout the book, was no lithe licra clad figure, but he had what was needed for the challenge – strength and determination. Jock had a famous shovel (perhaps the selfsame one that he slid down the Melantee pipes on) with sides welded on so he could fill a hundredweight sack in two scoops!

The Two Tenners !

One Fort William garage proprietor, Alex MacMillan (right), has good cause to remember that shovel - as a boy applying to Jock for a job, he was told very firmly, "fill that coal bag or go home!" But Alex was up to it and told me an interesting fact as he gave a handsome donation to the printing of "Up The Ben wi' Eddie"… His garage in Camaghael, the Clansman, was built from the old "Parade Garage" when it was dismantled in the High Street.

Still on the quest of who'd done *"multi-Bens"*, I heard that the lady on the right, 81 year old Ruby Irvine, had taken straw bales, one in each hand, up to the summit for the 1953 Coronation bonfire – 5 times! She could recall marshalling Scouts up The Ben – *"Obey your officer"* she remembers barking at them when they strayed from the path, but nothing about the straw bales. I had been warned she was too modest!

So you don't have to wield the ½ cwt shovel to be able to try the *"Charlie Anderson"*! Charlie himself is an ultrasonic operator on the West Highland Railway, he is also a part-time fire fighter so has the strength and, coming from Claggan, has the determination! Charlie contacted the Chambers and Miller families (opposite page with Charlie), who have children with cystic fibrosis, to tell them he was gathering over £1000 in sponsorship money for specialised toys and equipment for the kids. See the delight on their faces above when Charlie crossed the finishing line after his amazing four ups and downs. Going back 24hrs before that, here is the story as Charlie sets off on his record epic…

Leaving for his work on the Friday morning 1st October '04, Charlie found it was a nice day full of promise for his challenge to begin at 6.00 that evening. Sunshine turned to wind and rain, and that is how it remained throughout, falling as snow in the upper reaches. At 4.30pm Donna set off laden with hot food and dry clothes to administer from the top when Charlie would make his 4 (they had hoped 5 but it was atrocious conditions) appearances at the summit. She laid a trail of light sticks which burn for 12hrs to aid Charlie find the route. After Charlie had come and gone, Donna settled down in the shelter to wait for his second coming. A good advert for Nevis Radio, Donna spent the time listening to the radio and doing crosswords. When she zipped up to go to sleep, she found she'd to strike a balance between being frozen and soaking with condensation. Looking out of the shelter at one point, Donna found it all white. When Charlie arrived on his 2nd trip he told her that she might be having company as a man was heading up the path – the man didn't reach the summit, but reached the papers... *"Badly- equipped man rescued in atrocious weather"*! It was lucky for him that Charlie's supporters were able to assist after the man's phone call to the police that he was lost.

Photo courtesy
of Iain Ferguson

Meanwhile Charlie ploughed on up and down – *"mind over matter"* and *"head down and get on with it"* were phrases he used to describe the sheer determination. He will never forget the elation of walking into the stone building of the Ben Nevis Inn at 6.00pm on the Saturday as if he was in a scene from the Stella Artois ad! After a few of their products, Charlie was soon back at home snoring away contentedly. But Donna had to disturb him – because he was in the bath! Awakening the next day, Charlie felt fresh as he lifted his head off the pillow. Then he discovered the rest of his body stayed where it was!

The facts and figures are...

4.30pm – Donna sets off to light the way when darkness falls.

6.00pm – 10.30pm, Charlie goes up and down with supporter Alex Pryce.

11.00pm – 04.30am, 2nd up and down with John Mechie.

05.00am – 11.30am, Colin Ross from Corpach chums Charlie up and Donna returns with them from the summit.

12.30pm – 6.00pm, Charlie and Donna go up and down together with Phil Stevenson.

Some of the high spots of the 24hr epic were his companions, Donna with hot food and dry clothes, gusts of wind gliding him up the path. Some of the lows were the gusts when he changed direction on the zigzags and the gusts were now in his face! "I shall pick a better day next time," Charlie announced and Donna came back with, "What do you mean next time? You are on your own, pal!"

139

Now it can be told...

The 2004 Ben Nevis Race has come and gone. The thousand pounds, up for grabs for beating the Men and Ladies' records, is safely back in the Treasurer's pocket. As for my own aspirations, I was disappointed I did not win the draw for the lucky programme number! Record holders Kenny and Pauline Stuart started us off and Pauline's expression (right) seems to say, as she starts her watch, "Don't just stand there taking photographs – get a move on!"

But there is much to say before recounting the times and positions...

Pupils at Lochaber High School, under the wing of Leen Volwerk, took part in a poetry competition and the four prize-winning entries out of the 70 submitted were published in the programme – it bodes well for the future that there is such interest in the Ben. From left to right are Hannah Linton, Kirsty MacLennan, Elizabeth Collier teaming up with Iain Cameron, then Natalie Cottier. Here is Hannah reciting her poem...

Photo courtesy of Anthony MacMillan

The Ben Nevis Race by Hannah Linton

We gather ourselves at the start of the race
And my heart is pounding at such a brisk pace;
Stretching and bending we fight off the cold;
A race such as this is for none but the bold.
The old and the young all start together,
Dodging the rocks and running through the heather,
Slowly but surely we clamber uphill,
The task ahead will challenge my will.

Then I glimpse a runner from the corner of my eye,
Can I find the strength to stop them passing me by?
Gasping for breath and my legs feeling weak,
My eyes gaze upward looking for the peak.

Now through the clouds the summit's in sight,
Quickening my pace as I see the light;
I can hardly believe I'm nearing the top,
The pain I am feeling must surely stop.

Turning at the summit, no time to waste,
I must get down the mountain now with great haste;
As I come down my legs start to ease,
But gathering speed the pain moves to my knees.

Faster and fast running like mad,
Coming down with a speed I never knew I had;
Suddenly I pass a familiar face,
And as I cross the line – I've Won The Race!

Hannah Beth Linton

Dave Cannon at the moment of his fifth victory in the Ben Nevis Race, 1976, in a record time of 1hr 26mins 55secs.

Giving 4th place Natalie the last word in her "Oh No – the Ben Race Again"…

*Mankind pounding up my ancient face,
Taking part in this silly annual race.
I just really want to be left alone,
I am a very old extinct volcano.*

The first married couple to run in the Ben Race were Joan and Dennis Glass in 1975. Joan set a new Ladies' record time of 2hrs 17mins 50secs.

141

The 4th September 2004 dawned with perfect weather for the race – nice and warm in the park and a wind blowing us up the mountain with mist from halfway to keep you cool. On the starting line I introduced the "old" to the "new" with my pals from years gone by, Jim Smith and Harry Blenkinsop (below), both making this their last Ben Race and Ranger Ian Donaldson's daughters, Emmy and Nicky, who were having their first Ben after being inspired by seeing again the photo of their mum, Tordis, and dad embracing on the top – Ian was back in place this year to carry on the tradition with lips poised when I saw him as Nicky was coming up just behind me! Perhaps the sisters could have done with it wetter as they were swimming champions, but now they have their Ben Nevis certificates to add proudly to their medal collections.

A gathering of celebs! Kathleen the Champene, John – Eddie's son in law (unable to run after op.), Jean Ferguson looking after competitors' (and Nigel's) welfare, Ben veteran Phil Brown of Highland Hillrunners and Bob Dick, Cancer Research helper.

But what of the race itself and why no records broken?

One record was equalled by Ian Holmes of Bingley Harriers – that of Dave Cannon winning the Ben Nevis Race 5 times. Ian was this year's victor and now has won 5 times out of the 11 times he has competed. His time was 1hr 29mins 33secs, four minutes adrift of the record, while the first lady, Sharon Taylor also of Bingley Harriers, was 1hr 55mins 54secs, twelve and a half minutes outside the record. Times and places of those on this page are... Phil Brown, a very good 2hrs 06mins 18secs in 124th place, I was 263rd in 2hrs 31mins dead (?), closely followed by Nicky in 270th in 2hrs 32mins 14secs and sister Emmy in 312th place in 2hrs 42mins 41secs. Jim and Harry were taking my place at the bottom of the results, but can recall the glory days!

Ian Holmes said that while conditions were good, he was afraid they were not just right for record breaking. Next year!

2nd 1st 3rd

BEN NEVIS RACE 2004
39

BEN NEVIS RACE 2004
360

LOCHABER. A.C.
BEN NEVIS RACE 2004
148

And here are the top 3 – 2nd this year was last year's winner, Rob Jebb (above left), who became hooked on The Ben when watching his dad, Peter, and Ian Holmes (centre) running in the race – he couldn't wait to be old enough to enter! Rob usually wins the Lovat Scouts Trophy for 1st to the summit (it only takes him 57mins!).

Davy Rodgers (right) was cheered for winning the new memorial trophy for Jimmy Conn for the 3rd placed runner, which was Jimmy's best position back in the fifties. There was a huge hand for the runner with the "Over the Hill" tee shirt at the prize-giving as he was awarded his "Connochie Plaque" for his 21st Ben Race. He is Kevin Dobson, Bingley Harriers. Kevin's brother Frank brought up his own Connochie Plaque which he earned in 2001.

The right place at the right time

A chance remark can reveal another story in the life of The Ben - a typical example of how small the world is! Top Ten Ben runner, Dave Cummins of Shettleston Harriers, who with wife Fiona now live in Inverness, are standing beside Elaine and Tom Bagan from near Vancouver. Tom worked with Charlie Petrie when Charlie had emigrated to Canada after his great success in the "Golden Era" of the 50s. The Bagans were with a party of Scottish Country Dancers who had been having great weather for their Scottish tour until they visited Fort William! But never mind, for we were inside! Also there were Phyllis and Campbell Dixon from Nairn, Phyllis showing me that she can beat me at meringues as well as on The Ben! Dance teacher Norma MacLennan has made up a Scottish Country Dance called "A Day on The Ben" and it would be good fun to try it on the summit – ONE FINE DAY! In the meantime I'll collect more stories of our mountain – there are still many Ben Nevis people to see and tourists to chat to as we go *"Up The Ben wi' Eddie"*. You can just imagine Eddie saying in the picture below as he hands the baton over to me in the annual Great Glen relay race from Fort William to Inverness...

"You tell them, Jimmy. (gasp) You tell them about The Ben."

144

The final word of the chapter on records must go to the Master Roundsman of all time – Hugh Symonds (right), who sent the above photo of Eddie and says, *"Eddie on the Carn Mòr Dearg Arête on Sunday 20th May 1990 accompanying me on my Munro run."*

And what a run it was – Hugh (Ben winner in 1985) did every single Munro in Scotland, England, Ireland and Wales, 303 in one go!

Hugh went through 10 pairs of running shoes and had the company of 25 supporters at different times on the hills, completing it in an astonishing 97 days. Once, when he thought he was having to go alone, he woke up to find "a twiching bivvy sack surrounded by midges, labelled *'Here lies the body of Dermot McDonigle, please disturb.'"*

Roger Boswell kept Hugh's spirits up by telling him, *"It would be a nice day if it wasn't raining."* And Colin Donnelly, Ben winner in 1986, said of their abode for the night, *"It would be a good bothy if it had windows and a roof."*

Chapter 8
HISTORY OF THE OBSERVATORY

An Ascent of Ben Nevis in 1910

 Then suddenly the form of the Observatory grew out of the mist and the low outline of the Observatory Hotel seemed to rise up and strike one in the face. A few groping steps brought one to the door, and solitude was over then.

The little wooden room was full of wet steamy people, jostling with each other for cups of tea, and chattering at the pitch of their voices with nervous excitement. One thankfully shook off the desperate unreality of that overcrowded tea-house on the summit, the small steamed windows, the English voices, the cups and saucers, the stand of picture cards, and the leasee offering to stamp the same as proof of ascent. Outside the grey clinking stones were wet, the mist shrouded everything, and the Observatory, not ten feet away, stood in the half-light, a desolate monstrosity, through the enveloping drifts, the black and white of a snow bunting flitted noiselessly about the shuttered windows of the deserted pile.

Science has been sacrificed.

T.G., Glasgow Herald, Sept 9th 1910

147

Postcards from Heaven

OBSERVATORY HOTEL, BEN NEVIS

*"And they
call the
wind Maria."*

    A grand song for singing in the bath so you can get the deep notes reverberating! Guess who was the first to give names to storms like Ernest K. Gann's "Lazy Ethel"? It was none other than our own Clement Wragge. Here is an explanation of how Clement fits into things...

    Television weather presentation is so slick nowadays – showing little virtual showery clouds or shining suns on different areas as the camera zooms over counties, countries or the whole world. We know all about the forces of Mother Nature as the Earth spins round and round. But not so in the 1800s when weather experts began to investigate what happens in "Inner Space". Meteorology was becoming more sophisticated than the olden maps showing Ptholemei's cherubs!

    Societies round the world were coming round to the thought that the best way to study air streams would be to have mountain top observatories. The Scottish Meteorological Society already had plans to build a shelter on the summit of Ben Nevis so ideally placed, being a bastion of rock 4406 ft high, smack in the path of Atlantic storms. The Society had the most eminent of scientists and engineers.

    Thomas Stevenson, famous for lighthouses, designed a special screen to enable thermometers to be read in the extremely hostile conditions they would have to face. His son was the world famous novelist and poet, Robert Louis Stevenson, who in the same year was writing the immortal words in "Treasure Island" – "Arrrrrr, Jeem lad!" Alas for The Ben there was to be no fantasy of buried treasure, no riches beyond our wildest dreams. No Camelot! All that was on offer from the Government was £100 per annum on condition that the "stats" were made available to the Met Office. It was estimated it would cost £1,000 (a whole 100 copies of "Up The Ben wi' Eddie") to build the Observatory and £300 a year to run it. Traditionally observers worked for nothing, gathering data out of pure interest whilst doing everyday jobs. However up there on The Ben, the two observers and a cook were to be away from their families for ten months at a stretch and so had to be recompensed. So it all went on hold until the Society received a letter from Clement L. Wragge. Clement volunteered to take daily readings whilst his wife took simultaneous ones at sea level – just exactly what the Meteorological Society wanted. One of the aims of the Observatory was to study the difference in pressure readings between top and bottom, as they believed this might have been the key to accurate forecasting. The primary aim was to look out for approaching storms and to warn shipping so they could scurry for shelter. In those days ships were the lifeline of the nation as it says in the hymn on the top right...

So well thought of was maritime magnate David Hutcheson, the forerunner of MacBraynes, that the Observatory was to be called the Hutcheson Ben Nevis Observatory in his memory.

Meanwhile back at the Wragges, Clement and his wife, unaware they were going down in history, synchronised their watches and settled into a routine of readings:

Sea level	04.40
Halfway Loch	06.30
Spring★	08.15
Summit	09.00
··	09.30
··	10.00
Spring★	10.50
Halfway Loch	13.00
Sea level	15.00

The picture is of Clement and his Newfoundland dog, Renzo, in his shelter at the top – there was no shortage of stones! See if you can spot the ruins of his "howff" behind where the Observatory was built when you get up. It was a haven from the storms and a chance for him to have a brew up of coffee. The distinctive wooden strip in the walls is still there.

The heroic story of the "Inclement Wragge" caught the whole of Britain's attention. The papers featured him struggling through all kinds of weather with his pony,

> *The Earth belongs unto the Lord and all that it contains, Except for the Highlands and the Islands, and they belong to MacBraynes!*

Front cover of reprint of "Twenty Years on Ben Nevis" by Earnest Press.

which he left chomping on the grass at the Halfway Loch, whilst he and faithful Robin Renzo tackled the rest of The Ben. Money started pouring in! In a very short time The Ben was alive with road makers. The five mile road was constructed six feet wide and zigzagged so that it was never more than 1 in 5. Masons were building the Observatory with the summit blocks of granite. The race was on to be installed before winter took a grip and it took them only five months from start to finish. This included construction of the road, building bridges and the Observatory, all for a total cost of £2,031.08! By 17th October 1883, all was set for the grand opening – by a Campbell!

(If you are wondering who the time traveller is in the jacket and jeans on the right, the picture is of a BBC reconstruction of the party moving off to climb The Ben for the opening ceremony. Don't laugh, but requiring a wet day, they had to use fire hydrants to supply the rain!)

Mrs Campbell of Callart was landowner of the west side of The Ben, but no relation to Eddie! Clement wasn't given the post of Superintendent and went off to Australia to become Government Meteorologist.

That first winter spent on the summit was unbearable, and many alterations had to be made, including a giant tower so the Observers could get out from the snow (see picture on right!).

And so life settled down on The Ben and, with the road, came the tourists! A hotel was built alongside the Observatory on the summit. You can still see the remaining walled area just before you come to the Observatory. B&B came in at 10/- (50p), which was pricey, but then look at the trouble it would take to provide food and accommodation. For twenty-one years at the Observatory, readings were taken every hour on the hour, come rain, hail or shine unless something really dire happened like searching for a missing colleague which meant the 15.00 reading was taken at 15.03! The Observatory clock, pictured here, is a piece of history in itself, having gone round the world with Captain Cook, survived being shipwrecked and used in fixing the Mason-Dixon Line in America. The Observers soon became adept at taking a wind speed reading, measuring it by the extent they had to lean...

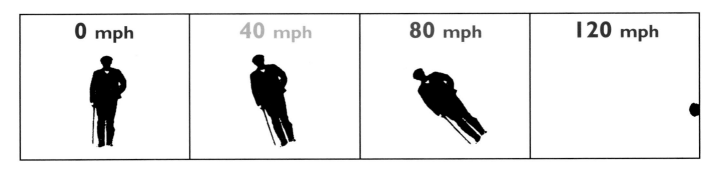

0 mph	40 mph	80 mph	120 mph

The spectre of closure hung constantly over the Observatory and, in spite of generous donations, supplemented by a 1/- (5p) levy on every tourist, funding was a continual problem. Not only was there the summit Observatory, but also the sea-level one, Glentower, which you can still see in the "Golden Mile" of Achintore Road – look for the pink tower.

The crunch came when the Treasury wouldn't match the £950 running costs. The last reading was entered in the log at noon on the 1st October 1904. The Observer wrote *"This day, by order of the Directors, observations were discontinued at this station."* Before putting down the date, he had looked up from the logbook to the calendar on the wall, as one does even although you know full well what the date is. He was utterly astonished to see the coincidence of the "thought for the day" for the 1st – ***"All things cometh to an end!"*** The hotel ran on for some years, then it too closed and the wind was left to blow and blow over the abandoned buildings. No one remained to observe the wonders of nature like the "Brocken Spectre" (red and blue rings round a person's shadow on a cloud). Great men of history had walked these summit stones – Edward Wymper of Matterhorn fame and Captain Scott's Antarctic team. P'raps when you're up there you can imagine, as the wind soughs around the thick walls of the ruins, you hear the distant reverberations of an Observer singing away happily in the tin bath in front of the stove

"The more it snows, tiddlypom!"

"Summit suds" by Morvern Skinner

BEN NEVIS OBSERVATORY - VISITORS BOOK

DATE	NAME	RESIDENCE	REMARKS	SUBS
1885				
Sept 30th	Annie C. Whyte	Fort William	Brought a storm up with me	
Oct 7	Mark McLoughlin	Inverlochy Cottage – do	Snow 4ft deep	
Oct 8	A. Lawrence Potch	Boston, Mass., USA		£5
Oct 23	Sir Richard Wallace MP	Inverlochy Castle	Walked up from Nevis Bridge in 3½	£10 ~~£5~~ ✗
Oct 23	J. K. Fitzhenry	Inverlochy Castle	Walked from Nevis Bridge 36 inches snow	
1886				
April 20	Arch. Mitchell	Oban	Road for most part impassable, Specially from loch. Depth of snow from 2 to 4 feet on road as far as it is distinguishable	
May 1st	John Whyte ⎫ Mrs Whyte ⎭	Library Hall Inverness	Honeymoon trip. Came up by the bridal path. (funny)	
..	Robina Whyte	Fort William	Twenty feet of snow on top	
..	William M. Whyte	Observatory Hotel	169th Ascent ⎫Weather	
June 1st	W. M. Whyte	.. ..	170th Ascent⎭ fine	
	Arch McIntyre	Easdsale	2nd Ascent by jove.	

"You're going to look through every entry! In how many years?"

Of course the West Highland Museum curator, Fiona Marwick (in photo) is correct, but after reading as many as I could in two days I began to think I knew the regulars - like Robina on 1st May in the extracts above. Each time she went up to the family hotel, she described her journey and finally, years later, she'd a tearful farewell to visit foreign climes.

I like the above entry – *"For the benefit of the disappointed ones…"*

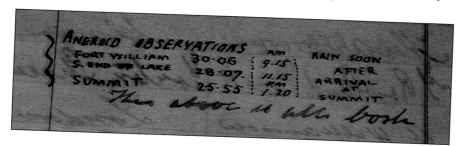

One kind visitor carefully noted these readings on his way up - only to be shot down in flames!

Some extracts were a bit political, depending what was happening in the world at the time and some used the book as a platform to advertise their products, like Samuel Austin of Birmingham – *"Wet wet wet, but thanks to Austin's 'Starch Spray' my collar has retained its stiffness though wet through."*

Surprisingly doctors had the most legible handwriting and a solicitor made me laugh with one entry: *"Horatius Bonar, W.S., Edinburgh, **staid** all night"* and underneath was written "Mrs Bonar, ditto"

Some famous family names appear, like the Muggerages and the Observers would also record their comings and goings – W. T. Kilgour came up with his 6 year old son Willie accompanied by A. C. Mossman who was having his 27th ascent in August '02. The number of times making the climb featured a lot with some multi-ones -

William Stewart, 367th ascent.
James McGregor, Fort William, 60th ascent, 2hrs 10mins (with 4 loaves on my back).
James Rankin, Tomacharrich, 80th ascent in season.

Rather a lot of people wrote *"1st ascent (and last!)"* with James Caldwell of Paisley writing *"1st offence"*!!!

Beaumont Burrell was on his 10th ascent whereas Rosalie Burrell had written a few days earlier *"WILL **NEVER** COME BACK"* – but she did!

William Whyte of the hotel recorded his many many ascents in beautiful script…

 As you can see on the top of the photo of the Visitors' Book on the previous page, William wrote the amount of visitors to the summit for each season – 2800 in 1885. For the month of July 1886, he recorded 11 dry days with 2 good views and 310 visitors, 20 wet days with 190 visitors, 110 ladies out of 500 (but who's counting).

Many log entries spoke of how people were dreading the descent: "Very tired – don't know how I am going to get back down." Sarah Black from Appin solved that by coming in a wheelbarrow! Lionel Ford of Cambridge bemoaned the fact that Miss Jessica Ford needed a horse at 21/- (£1.05). Visitors often wrote in praise of their ponies and guides – *"able to commend our lad and pony Jane."* Poet's Corner was much to the fore with offerings like Peter McIntyre's from Fort William:

The climb was hard, the view, a treat
If 'twere not for the rain and sleat
For fog this mountain can't be beat
"No water, thanks, I take mine "neat"

153

going
going

gone !

Oh, there it is !

"Not a lot of people know that !"

The John Muir Trust took over The Ben in April 2000, but the highest square feet in the land where the shelter is belongs to the Lochaber Mountaineering Club. The deeds are in the vaults of the bank, but I don't know if they have insurance against the snow disappearing in summer as the legend has it (see "myths and legends" at the start of Cammy's story in "The Racing Section").

Members of the club decided the refuge shelter in the ruins of the Old Observatory wasn't "user friendly" enough in many respects and put up a nice new one as the photo (below right) shows, with Ranger Ian putting the finishing touches.

You'll notice the plaque in the middle of the Observatory wall:

These are the remains of the
METEOROLOGICAL OBSERVATORY
which, with the path from Achintee, was built in 1883
with publicly subscribed funds. It was managed by the
SCOTTISH METEOROLOGICAL SOCIETY
and representatives of the
ROYAL SOCIETIES of LONDON & EDINBURGH.
hourly observations were maintained for 21 years
and sent by telegraph via Fort William to
meteorological services throughout Europe.
The Brocken Spectre seen from here on cloud in the
Great Corrie by C.T.R. Wilson in 1894 led him to
Researches which culminated in the development
Of the Wilson Cloud Chamber, and for which he was
Awarded a Nobel Prize in 1927.

In the unveiling ceremony for the plaque on 27th July 1969, Miss Wilson, who was Professor Wilson's daughter, spoke of how her father felt privileged to have had *"the opportunity to see the beautiful coloured coronas and glories, a striking aspect of the infinite beauty of Nature."* She also went on to compliment Dr Thom and Mr Farman for carrying up the heavy plaque and for fixing it without anywhere to plug in a drill!

Always one to name drop, I must tell you that my doctor in Peebles was the cousin of Miss Rosamund Wilson and he was also present at the ceremony. The late Dr Robin Wilson was an artist and he painted this beautiful picture for me "The First Snow", displaying it in an exhibition before it came time for my birthday!

At the signing in before the start of the Ben Nevis Race, runners are given a souvenir miniature of "Dew of Ben Nevis" whisky. One year I gave mine to Dr Wilson thinking he'd give it pride of place on his mantelpiece, but he straight away used it for more medicinal purposes!

The First Snow - Ben Nevis

"..and now for the weather"

Gazing at this wonderful oil painting by Jimmy Johnston makes you feel that you are right up there with the Observer taking the readings – from the comfort of your favourite armchair beside a roaring fire while the wind and rain is battering at the window!

Visitors beseechingly enquire about when the best time is to go up The Ben to get a nice day for a view. Let's see what can be gleaned from the records that they kept while the Observatory was operating...

Facing facts – The Ben is wet! 240,000 tons of water fell one year on the summit! Only a hundred clear days in the year and winds can blow, as Wm Kilgour states quietly, *"probably at the rate of 2½ miles a minute"* – that is **ONE HUNDRED AND FIFTY MILES AN HOUR!**

William also talks about the dryness of the air being "not even equalled in the heart of the Arabian Desert". Everyone says to me "Pull the other one – it plays Annie Laurie" when I recount that one year in the race, the sweat didn't drip off your brow, it just evaporated in a haze. The proper name for that, as I learnt from Ken Crocket's book is "sublimed" where the banks of snow can vaporise - disappearing without first turning into water.

Temperaturewise the summit is usually about 15°F (8°C) lower than in Fort William, but sometimes it can get really hot - the hottest being 67°F (19°C) in the shade one June day and whole weeks of 130°F (54°C) in the direct summer sunshine. In those conditions the Observers couldn't do their usual sunbathing on the roof as the lead got too hot! You may be surprised to see

TABLE I.—Ben Nevis Monthly Values, 1884 (Rainfall, 1885) to 1903.

Month.	Barom. at 32°. (Inches).	Temperature, (° Fahr.).						Rainfall. (Inches).						Sunshine. (Hours).								Cloud per cent-age.	Wind Force. Scale, 0—12.
	Mean.	Mean.	Warmest Year.		Coldest Year.			Mean.	Wettest Year.		Driest Year.			Mean.	% of possible	Best Year.		Worst Year.				Mean.	Mean.
Jany.,	25·221	24·0	28·8	'88	17·5	*'95		18·33	35·32	'00	3·42	'97		22·4	10	69·6	'88	3·1	'94			88	2·9
Feby.,	25·228	23·8	30·6	'91	18·7	*'95		13·55	36·24	*'03	2·85	'86		42·3	16	86·5	'91	4·9	*'03			83	2·7
March,	25·163	24·0	28·5	*'93	20·0	*'91		15·25	37·95	*'03	3·84	'00		54·7	15	105·5	'92	10·8	*'03			84	2·5
April,	25·295	27·6	34·9	*'93	24·1	*'91		8·48	20·22	'00	2·50	'91		80·4	19	150·6	'93	32·5	'98			80	2·3
May,	25·411	33·0	38·9	'96	26·9	*'85		7·90	15·81	'02	2·91	'96		116·3	23	238·8	'01	31·7	'85			78	2·0
June,	25·468	39·7	45·7	'87	35·4	*'85		7·54	14·66	'90	1·94	*'89		127·0	22	249·8	'88	24·1	'90			77	1·8
July,	25·437	41·1	47·8	'01	37·1	'90		10·79	15·22	'99	4·09	*'89		84·8	16	170·2	'97	24·2	'95			86	1·6
Aug.,	25·360	40·4	48·7	'99	37·6	'03		13·35	20·97	'03	5·58	'99		58·1	13	†212·5	'99	8·7	'89			88	1·7
Sept.,	25·372	38·0	43·3	'95	34·4	{'92 *'85}		15·74	43·54	'91	1·32	*'94		69·3	16	126·4	*'94	12·4	'99			83	2·1
Oct.,	25·231	31·4	36·3	*'97	26·4	*'85		15·42	37·30	'90	4·67	*'94		41·8	13	90·8	*'94	14·3	'93			85	2·5
Nov.,	25·286	28·9	33·6	*'97	25·8	'93		15·36	32·48	'99	7·86	'02		27·8	11	58·8	'96	8·1	'88			85	2·7
Dec.,	25·110	25·2	28·4	'00	20·1	'86		19·07	48·34	'00	3·75	'90		18·0	9	35·1	'92	1·1	'93			87	2·7
Mean Annual,	25·300	31·4	33·0	'93	29·7	{'85 '86 '92}		160·78	240·13	'98	107·85	'86		735·9	16	969·2	'88	508·9	'03			84	2·3

* Note how frequently two consecutive months furnish "records," showing prolonged spells of unusual weather.
† Only one other August with an average of over 20 per cent. of the possible—118 hours, in 1885.

that it does not get arctic-type cold, although it certainly might feel it with the wind chill factor! The coldest recorded on the summit was on 6th Jan 1894 at only half a degree away from 0°F (-17.4°C), whereas a temperature as low as -17°F (-26°C) was recorded at Braemar.

So to answer the thorny question "When should I climb The Ben to be sure of a good day with a view?" – It's like the time we asked a policeman in Malaga where we could park and his reply was "You know the lottery numbers?"

Feed all the info into the computer and "hey presto" out come the results, but like all good forecasts there is always a "perhaps" and all through the book I'm reminding you that you have to be prepared for the worst at any time of the year. Even on the hottest, sunniest day in the race we have to carry full body protection and whistle in case of sudden weather change or getting into difficulties.

Here are the pie charts for you to pick and mix...

The Sunshine Hours

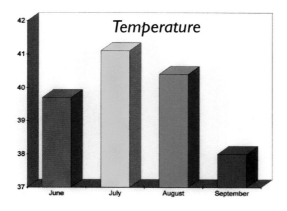

September

August

July

June

127 hrs

Go with green and the leader is June with 127 hours of sunshine in the month – poor August is not very tourist-friendly at only 58.1.

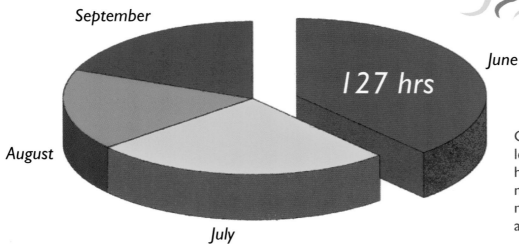

July slightly in the lead with 41.1°F (5°C) but June is back as the driest month with a mere 7,540 tons of rain!

July scores again with the least gales by far and June afternoons can be prone to fog.

So June and July are the front runners but remember, too, that the last of these readings were taken 100 years ago and there have been climatic changes since. As you can see from the photo I'm investing heavily in global warming if it should ever reach the summit! What would Jimmy Johnston's Observer think today, as he makes his way back to the building for a warming cuppa?

JIMMY'S PLACE
SUNBEDS FOR HIRE

Don't do as I do,
do as I say !

Weather on The Ben is a bit like wedded bliss – "Darling this" and "Darling that" first thing in the morning, then by lunchtime it all goes pearshaped. So be sure to have plenty warm and waterproof stuff to put on like the two Canadian ladies pictured below with two other climbers...

The *sunshine* of your *smile* !

The Canadian ladies on the right were leaving the summit in shorts as I went up and they said how nice it was to see someone else in shorts as I came towards them. Meeting them again on the way down they'd donned their waterproofs, seeing the nasty rain had come on. They laughed when I said I wanted a picture of an unpleasant afternoon!

24hrs in the life of a Ben runner

Old Father Time waits for no man

Cartoon courtesy of "Up and Down" magazine

And, as you will have guessed, that picture in the yellow shorts on the previous page was of me over 30 years ago. There are cut-off times at different stages in the race and if you fall short you're sent back. Very necessary because you don't want runners out too long and possibly getting into difficulties in September with it getting dark and cold at nights. The times are:

Start at Claggan Park to Red Burn	-	1 hour
.. .. to Summit	-	2 hours
.. .. to Finish	-	3hrs 15mins

All this is getting round to saying that I am beginning to draw near to those times and sought out the very man who could help – none other than the head of the mighty Brooks Dynasty of Ben Runners, Graham. Overlord of the Swimming Pool Leisure Centre, Graham dispenses advice and writes great stories (as you see throughout this book) for "Lochaber Life", the monthly magazine for Fort William residents. We explored every avenue, but had to discard such useful tips as *"pick up a small stone and roll it back down shouting 'ROCK!' causing everyone to scatter! Or offer round barley sugars and you'll be twenty yards up by the time they unwrap them!"* None of these cunning ploys would gain me those elusive minutes and it seemed that I was doomed. That was until I got a card from the doctor and everything was about to change. It was an invite to a *"Well Man"* check up...

"Cough." said the doctor as I winced at the cold hand.

In between the various tests, the doc was asking me how my running was going.

"I was disappointed," I told her, *"with my Ben Nevis time this year."*

"What do you take during the race?" she enquired as she drew off some blood for the Cholesterol check.

"Nothing really," I explained, *"but I do carry a Mars bar in case I run out of steam."*

"A Mars bar! That is thinking from the 1960s!" She pushed her glasses further up her nose and looked me straight in the eye continuing, *"I can take 10 minutes off your time on The Ben."*

"T-t-ten minutes!" my eyes lit up with the old fervour, *"Did you just say 10 whole minutes?"* It was like her saying 10 more years of running The Ben!

"All you have to do is to swallow a couple of these "Trinitroglucerine" capsules as the race progresses – it is all perfectly legal."

I only half heard her go on to say that the one drawback was that it made you celibate.

"That's no problem!" I laughed as I seized the packet and gobbled one down, *"The office party is coming up on Saturday."*

She gave me a puzzled look.

Later that night I realised I'd misheard the doctor when I thought she'd said *"celebrate"* and was somewhat humbled as I sat toying with my soldiers of toast at breakfast the next morning. I suddenly sat bolt upright when my eyes lit on an advert in the Lochaber News. Next moment I grabbed the car keys and was on my way to the vets! It was the perfect solution – *"Diagra"* – a second-generation digital product that was being experimented on stallions.

"Yes yes" I said wearily as the vet went on and on about the stuff, warning me that my horse might experience a secondary spasm. My only thought was get out and into the car. When at last there, I hastily swallowed two of the tablets.

Remember that warning about the secondary spasm? Well, I couldn't get home quick enough and kind of stretched an amber traffic light on the roadworks at Spean Bridge. It would have been no bother but for a police car sitting watching. That too was no bother, although they gave me that very pained and penetrating look that police do as I went past. At that selfsame moment the famous secondary spasm kicked in – between two of my fingers. They shot apart in a V formation.

*Thanks to clipart
for illustrations*

The police pulled me in before I'd even reached the end of the roadworks and were walking towards me with that *"Right, Chummy!"* expression. Luckily they laughed when they saw my predicament, but gave me a stern warning to watch where I was going.

Everybody and everything seems to have an extra oar to put in these days! Much relieved, I was into gear and away – straight into the biggest hole you've ever seen.

The fire brigade didn't take too long to come and soon the clippers and burners were getting me out. I was transferred to a helicopter and we droned our way to the Belford Hospital.

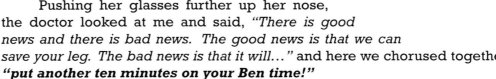

Pushing her glasses further up her nose,
the doctor looked at me and said, *"There is good
news and there is bad news. The good news is that we can
save your leg. The bad news is that it will..."* and here we chorused together,
"put another ten minutes on your Ben time!"

"*Stout heart to a stae brae*"

Little Emily clambers up to join the rest of her family, sister Matilda and mum and dad Tordad and James – Tordad coming from the old East Germany.

The title words above were uttered by William Kilgour when he set off with a friend to visit the Observers on the summit, little knowing that soon "the Plateau of Storms" was going to live up to its name and almost claim their lives. Here is the vivid description William gives in "20 Years on Ben Nevis"…

In winter, visitors were always welcomed at the Observatory, and not having been aloft for some time previous, the writer, accompanied by a friend, resolved upon a nocturnal climb in December. The night was an ideal one for such an exploit – so a wire from the top informed us, and when we commenced the ascent about five o'clock a full moon rode in an almost cloudless sky, whilst the road being frost-bound was easy to walk upon, and our spirits were high as we set stout hearts to a stae brae. All went well till we reached the tarn, but here Dame Nature began to treat us with scant courtesy.

In a twinkling, fog enveloped the hill, but

Stout heart indeed

this did not disturb us greatly as we meant to stick to the path, which, so far, we had experienced no difficulty in following. On we trudged, steadily mounting; but hark! what was that ominous sound? Wind, by Jove! and with power in its sough; we could hear the storm coming adown the corries. "Keep up your pluck, old chap," said I to my companion, but next moment my own courage fell a degree or two as a swish of snow caught our faces. Then all of a sudden we were at the mercy of the wind, buffeted, half blinded with snow-drift, and hardly able at times to get out of the spot.

When the storm broke, we had accomplished about two-thirds of the journey, and to give up then would have been galling, so we determined to proceed. Very soon icicles depended from our hair and moustaches, while the snow coalesced on the exposed sides of our faces. By this time our progress was very slow in consequence of our garments having become frozen stiff, and we could not, do what we liked, bend either our arms or our legs. Unconsciously there crept over us that almost irresistible desire to lie down and sleep, of which travellers tell us, but we fought strenuously against the temptation. The tempest shewed no signs of abating, and to make matters worse, we discovered to our horror that we had got off the path — an error easier committed than remedied.

Try as we might, no path could we find, and the awful truth that we were lost — lost on Ben Nevis, dawned upon us. Leaning on our sticks we groaned, and so utterly worn out were our bodies that it was only with the greatest difficulty we could maintain an upright position. Would that balmy sleep of death come soon, and when our stiffened corpses were discovered, who would break the news to our loved ones down below?

"Halloo!" Simultaneously our ears caught the sound, and in one voice we echoed back the gladsome shout. Soon we saw the glimmer of a lamp, and next instant one of the observers was grasping each of us by the hand. His presence seemed to put new life into us, and learning that we were only about 500 feet below the Observatory, we exerted our remaining stamina and at length reached that haven of rest. 'Twas a narrow squeak, and until the inevitable intervenes, I have no desire to obtain again so close a view of the Valley of the Shadow.

The way markers on the Plateau of Storms lead the way to Home Sweet Home

Photo courtesy of the Royal Meteorological Society

"I have on my desk in front of me a small but historic piece of cable..."

It was thus that I started a 5000 word short story for The Canongate Prize. As it happens, I was unplaced, but no matter, it is the taking part! The story is a fantasy. The hero is obsessed with anything connected with Ben Nevis and attempts to use a bit of the inner core of the old telegraph cable stretching down The Ben to wire up a table lamp. When he awakes from the resultant explosion, he finds himself back in the early 1900s when the cable was still shiny and new. Love interest is supplied by "Nurse Strudel", but I won't spoil the ending for you, except to say he has a terrible job trying to explain to his wife!

The real story of the telegraph cable is very interesting as it was at a time when electricity was in its infancy. Who all have heard of the "farad" – electromagnetic unit of capacity? I recall a textbook on the subject that was so old, it stated in a passage that "Young Faraday is doing good work in this field"! Michael Faraday invented the electric motor and he would have been the first to go and study the ghostly readings that were surging up and down the Ben Nevis cable at different times of the day, but he had died before the Observatory had been built – his friends always warned him he was working too hard!

Pigeon post was the order of the day before the huge marine armoured cable was laid to the summit to get weather reports down to the newspapers. During the summer months the telegraph was in great demand from the tourists all eagerly wanting to send funny messages to their loved ones. On the Pony Track you won't see much of the cable, as it runs straight down the Red Burn, but if you scout about in the ruins of the Observatory, you will see where it terminates at what was the telegraph office. The Observers found that a separate wire had to be run alongside the cable to establish a better "earth" – the staff were quite used to getting electric shocks jumping out at them from anything metal when the air was highly charged. In conditions such as this, things would start to buzz and the Observers' hair stand on end. To see this in the dark must have been spectacular with St Elmo's Fire sparkling out from raised up fingertips! I was reporting to friends that I'd been covered in an inch wide strip of deep purple light when running down The Ben through the mist and snow. Too much exposure to that (they said) causes one to change sex!

One June afternoon in 1895, it got so dark that the Observatory staff could see that something above and beyond your normal storm was brewing. The cook left the kitchen for fear of all the sparks coming from the metallic objects. He had just sat himself in the office when the whole Observatory was lit up by a blinding flash of lightning and deafened by a thunderous explosion. The cook landed unconscious and the Observatory went on fire! They all rallied round with water and snow and quickly had it out, but the telegraph instrument was "toast"! When cookie awoke he was still in the 1890s so had nothing to explain to the wife!

P'raps it was after this that the "Faraday Cage" was built wherein, it is said (see note 1), the staff could crouch in safety till the storm passed.
Note 1: presumably said by the same people who say the Halfway Loch was built to supply the porridge factory inside Melantee!

Another 'Met' weekend in Fort William !

"When Thor displays his mighty rage, 'tis time to hit the Faraday Cage!"

Visitors point to the metal structure behind the Observatory and wonder what it might have been... Nothing so glamorous as the refuge for the Observers to sit in while bolts of lightning were miraculously deflected! "It was merely," Marjory Roy said, crouching in the cage with John Pottie, "a lockable store where Clement Wragge could leave his stuff free from little Victorian fingers before the Observatory was built!"

John is the measurer of all-year-round snow banks and Marjory is the retired Superintendent of the Edinburgh Met Office. They'd come up, as 21 years ago, with a group to raise a glass to the memory of "The Weathermen of Ben Nevis 1883 – 1904". This time, alas, to commemorate the hundredth anniversary of the closure of the Observatory. The two day meeting in Fort William, Friday 11th and Saturday 12th June '04, celebrated the achievements of the Observatory during its 21 year existence. Marjory has written the "Weathermen" book and gave an illustrated talk to a packed audience, showing us just what conditions the Observers had to face – at times so bad that Clement Wragge's dog turned back! The theme of the other talks was global warming, including Davy Austin of Nevis Range's amazing footage of the 1992 floods in the Ben Nevis area – you can picture local residents rowing furiously after the barrels of whisky floating down the River Lochy! On the Saturday we toasted the old Observers at the summit.

Following the walk up The Ben on the Saturday, everyone had a healthy appetite for the lovely meal in the restaurant up Aonach Mor – via gondola!

"Cruinn 'an ceann a cheile air mullach na beinn a's airde 'san Rioghachd so..."
("Assembled together on the summit of the highest mountain in this kingdom...")

1902 Coronation telegram

Slàinte (cheers!)

12th June '04,...

...a day of days in the life of The Ben, and it started for our party at 7.30 am – not the earlier start we made 21 years ago, but then we are all that bit older! As befitting a team of meteorologists, the weather came good as predicted and we had a nice warm day although into the mist on the upper slopes. The sun broke through on the summit but no views of Ireland as I been hoping for as I'd got my telescope – first time since 1968!

On the right is the scene as we pass **Eddie's bench**, with Richard Tabony of the Met Office leading the way. Dick's talk on Friday was *"Changes in weather over Scotland since 1961 – an illustration of Global Warming?"*. There was no doubt that temperature trends are on the way up and it was asked what we should do about Scottish skiing in the future – *"Go to the Alps!"*

Speaker Davy Austin concurred with that and added that he used to mark in his logbook at Nevis Range, "wrong type of snow" – now, he said, any kind of snow would be welcome!

Behind Dick in the photo is Roger Wild who is Mountain Safety Advisor of The Mountaineering Council of Scotland. Roger came with us to the top and then went off to see how Mick Tighe (on the left in photo on the right) was getting on coming up with Richard Lamb and his friends. In 2001 Richard's climbing companion, Neil Stoodley, fell to his death on The Ben and Richard had lost a leg and most of his fingers in the 1,000-foot fall. Returning to Ben Nevis to pay tribute to his friend Neil, Richard chose to get to the top via Tower Ridge, raising £10,000 for The Limbless Association and Disability Sports! Roger Wild went on past them down the ridge and looked in at the CIC hut to have a cuppa with Alex and Mary Gillespie, who were filming with Norwegians. £10,000 was also mentioned by four lads (right) who were climbing The Ben in aid of "Cry in the Dark", a Romanian Orphanage. This was their first stage in doing the 3 Peaks. Many other groups were represented and further up The Ben we came across another well-known Ben Nevis man...

Photo courtesy of Iain Ferguson

Jeff   Richard   Iain   Peter

...George Bruce !

Just two more quick stories about George before telling you about the imposing jacket...

In the days when the 10p in the last story with George and Prince Charles would have been known as 2/-, George and Donald Watt were beating a retreat from the high tops in life threatening weather conditions. The wind tore at their anoraks forcing them to crawl on all fours and the cold was beginning to seep into their very souls – then George found two bob (10p)! Then a shilling – a threepenny bit – a sixpence. By now he was crawling away from their escape route, heading back up the hill. By the time Donald reached him it looked doubtful if they could survive much longer, but by this time George had amassed 17/6. Donald shouted in his ear above the screaming blizzard, *"If you come back now, I'll make it up to a pound!"*

The same pair, both highly respected members of the rescue team, were in the news for many months for seeing a cottage at Loch Mullardoch, which vanished as they approached. I got George to retell the story to the Met party as we chatted to him on The Ben, having us in fits of laughter as he demonstrated the lie detector test he had to submit to where his right arm would start flapping if he was telling "porkies"!

George was on The Ben on that 12th June day as part of the huge fund-raising organisation which run the "Four Peaks Challenge". They had started on Thursday and had done Slieve Donard in Northern Ireland, Snowdon in Wales, Scafell Pike in England and were now almost finished on The Ben – just a few more to come past on their way down. George is standing at "John's Wall" and cheery John himself was marshalling lower down. The pair had accompanied the walkers throughout the whole journey and were looking forward to getting home to lunch!

Bidding George farewell, we came on more sponsored ones, the various groups differentiating themselves with labels, tee-shirts or orange tape round rucksacks for the benefit of their marshals to check them through the various points on the hill.

Finding a piece of the Observatory lightning conductor (Photo courtesy of Iain Ferguson)

Splitting the girls in two is Chris. They are a joint group of 40 of lawyers and accountants climbing The Ben for Cancer Research and planning to have a much-deserved party afterwards!

The telescope was quite a source of amusement for visitors on the Pony Trail and I was asked if I was looking to see the Loch Ness Monster! One of the most frequently asked questions to the old Observers was, "Can we look through your telescope?"

They didn't have one, as it wasn't, as so many thought, an Astronomical Observatory – a bit too much in the clouds for that!

At the top were more "Ben Nevis notables" – Donald Paterson and Harry Campbell from the rescue team. They had been guiding up the "orange" group, being sponsored for Macmillan Cancer Relief. Another lot had kilts and St Andrews Cross tee shirts and were much photographed, but had dispersed before I changed the memory stick in my camera! Donald is a strong runner as you can see from the picture below of the start of the Cow Hill race outside the Alexandra Hotel. Number 278 is John O'Neil and I think the only time I beat him in The Ben Race was the year Elvis died and the heart was knocked out of him!

mist mist and more mist

Harry   Me   Donald

Photo courtesy of Anthony MacMillan

168

Goodbye

Goodbyes were said and we gathered our stuff to go back down to leave The Ben for more groups to come up its famous Pony Track and get their photos taken smiling on the trig point. To stand up there means so much to so many people. Our party's average age was "pretty high" with only one youngster and the Headmaster of the school below was pointing that out to me – not many young ones on The Ben. Mr Peter Phillips, Headmaster of Cundall School in North Yorkshire brings his 6th form pupils up The Ben each year and he kindly gave me a hand over the stile with the telescope – I had the feeling it would have been no problem for him to wheech both me and the telescope over! It really was a delight to see the kids run off excitedly back to their minibus. Peter is a piper and had taught the son of the baronial Clerk family of my hometown, Penicuik. Perhaps the boys and girls in the photo will return for the 150th anniversary of the Observatory's closure in 2054 and will rest at **Eddie's Bench** and watch young ones go by, who in their turn will return in 2108!

Don't say "cheese", say "MIDGES!"

Maybe by that time someone will have found the 10p George Bruce dropped – but all will, I hope, remember **Eddie**.

Alex rose one evening...

...and wiped the frost from his bedroom window, a bit like Good King Wenceslas upon the Feast of Stephen. "Come and see this, Mary!" he shouted.

Photo courtesy of Alex Gillespie

They stood in awe at the sight. Had it been over one hundred years ago, the pair might have set out bearing victuals for those on duty in the Observatory on the top. Now there's no one, but there are memories – powerful, strong ones. Memories of names from the past and names from the present. The Ben looks fondly down on the town where the folk from Fort William and surrounds lie sleeping. In the morning, unaware of the influence the mountain has over everyone, they will greet each other with the words:

"*Grand day for goin' up The Ben wi' Eddie!*"

Thankyou

Sharon says a
BIG THANK YOU
for your £10 going to cancer
research and special thanks
to all those listed on the next
page who made this possible
with their help in printing
"Up The Ben wi' Eddie"

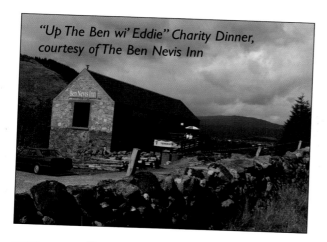
"Up The Ben wi' Eddie" Charity Dinner,
courtesy of The Ben Nevis Inn

Iain Ferguson's photo of The Poachers' Ball

Thankyou

Nevisprint, Lochaber School of Motoring, Caledonian Hotel, Clan Macduff Hotel, Altonside GH, Minaig, Alt-an-Lodge, Beaufort, The Willows, Oak Bank, Glenaladale, Westhaven, Buccleugh, Myrtyle Bank, Cruachan, Locheil, Fassfern, Melantee, Glenburn, Ronald Campbell Roofing, Clansman Garage, Lochy Bar, Mind The Craic Productions, Slipways Auto, Hebridean Jewellery, Hotscot, Claggan Stores, Easydrive, Travis Perkins, Highland Industrial Supplies, Marshall & Pearsons, Ellis Brigham staff, Inverness Insurance Centre (Donald Fraser), J&M McIntosh, Newco, McConechys, The Nevis Centre, Letterfinlay Foods Ltd, Rafford Films, Ben Nevis Distillery, Burnside Garage, An Drochaid, Lochaber Leisure Centre, Celtic FC, Rangers FC, Morrisons, The Beauty Room, MacDonald Bros, Murray Fiddes Transport Training, Alex Allan Insurance, Lochaber Rural Complex, D. Rodgers Slater, Limetree Studio, Caledonian MacBrayne, Allan Ingram Industrial Cleaners, Printsmith, and many others.

Marjory's Daffodil Teas

It was a real "feel good" factor to meet these companies and to hear as in the words of Robert Proven of Letterfinlay Foods it made his day to talk about Eddie. Many many individuals gave donations and are summed up by Henrietta Mackinnon of Kinlochleven who said as girls they went to the "Braxie" hall at Inverlochy for the Saturday night dancing and Eddie would tell them to start walking home - he would then finish his taxi customers, catch the girls up and take them home. Associations have been most generous with the Highland Council, The Ben Nevis Race Association, The Nevis Partnership, the Masons, North Kessock Scottish Dance Club and the lottery grant from "Awards for All". The Ben Nevis Inn put on a wonderful fund-raising dinner. Roybridge Hall saw two fund-raising dances a Scottish Country dance (see right!) and the Poachers' Ball. There have been raffles, quizzes and Marjory's Daffodil teas. Still to come is the Billy Brooks Memorial race after Billy's sad death. Also coming shortly is the "Beat the hour for Eddie" relay race following the route of the Ben Nevis Race up and down The Ben from Claggan Park and the intriguingly titled "Tina and Lyn's Jail Break". And more and more donations, but it is time now to stop collecting and to hand over to Mike of Nevisprint to wave his magic wand and turn this into a book!

Billy's Memorial Race

the DUKE of PERTH

(courtesy of Tony Milne, Edgereelers)